n

LAKE LADOGA

SUOJÄRVI

SORTAVALA

VALAM

LENINGRAD

JOENSUU

NURMES

TERJOKI

VIIPURI

Vuoksi R.

IMATRA

PUNKAHARJO

SAVONLINNA

NARWA

SOTKAMO

IISALMI

MIKKELI

LAPPEENRANTA

RISTIINA

KAJAANI

HOGLAND

FINLAND

KUOPIO

HAMINA

KOTKA

IISUKKA

VAAJAKOSKI

HEINOLA

LAHTI

LOVISA

KARSTULA

PORVOO

KEURUJ

JYVÄSKYLÄ

JÄMSA

PÄLKÄNE

HATTULA

HELSINKI

GULF OF

TALLINN

HIMANKA

LAPUA

VIRRAT

RUOVESI

HÄMEENLINNA

TAMMISAARI

PIETARSAARI

KANGASALA

KURIKKA

TAMPERE

HANKO

NAANTALI

WAASA

KRISTINESTAD

PORI

Kokemäki R.

TURKU

RAUMA

GULF OF BOTH

GULF OF BOTHNIA

ALAND IS.

T. E. HANLEY
COLLECTION

✛

Friedsam
Memorial Library

✛

FINLAND: LAND OF HEROES

TOIVO ROSVALL
has also written

THE VERY STUPID FOLK
A Finnish Tale

Illustrated by
TIBOR GERGELY

Published by
E. P. DUTTON & CO., INC.

FINLAND:
LAND OF HEROES

By

TOIVO ROSVALL

→»» «««←

*With an Illustrated Supplement
and Endpaper Map*

NEW YORK
E. P. DUTTON & CO., INC.
1940

TO
BERNARD ROSS

CONTENTS

FINLAND: LAND OF HEROES

I ∽

ALWAYS YESTERDAY

A LITTLE spring forces its way out of the rock and
soil in a hillside park above the city of Turku, the
old capital of Finland. So little does it attract your
attention that you turn away to look at the city at
your feet: a city stretched out in a long valley, with
a river wandering through the middle, feeling resigned that its freedom has been hemmed by the
stone embankments, its wildness curbed by rows of
trees. The streets are straight; they meet each other
at right angles, with business-like precision. After a
time even such materialistic streets waver: they lose
their determination to push on ruthlessly and finish
their pattern with a romantic flourish: they are so
overawed by the dynamic personality of the cathedral at the river bank and by the forcefulness of the
castle at the mouth of the river, a castle looking grim
and forbidding even in the lush meadow which sur-
rounds it, that they do not dare to go beyond these
sentinels at either end but remain content to keep
humbly within bounds. Near-by hills close in the
valley to make absolutely clear to the streets that
they shall not go farther—somewhat like Heidelberg,
except that here there are no vineyards covering the
hillsides, that instead of the *Philosophenweg* here

FINLAND

is only a spring gushing out of the rock and soil on the hillside. An ordinary spring—peer as closely as you like, there is nothing unusual about it.

Down below, the big dusky red cathedral has seen men worshiping God for seven centuries: men have died defending its treasures and its beliefs from the enemy; now they lie at rest within its walls, convinced that they have lived justly and died nobly. Farther away, the big, square gray castle has lived the history of Finland for an equally long time; its very stones seem to breathe in anguish, seeking for a voice which could tell of the intrigues, the innocent deaths, the loves and glories they have sheltered and thus release them from that anguish. But the spring—the water always bubbles up sparkling and gay, forgetting altogether that eight hundred years ago St. Henry baptized the Finns in this same spring and made them Christians, forgetting that for many centuries before St. Henry's crusading zeal came to disturb its peace, there was life on the banks of the river below.

While Babylon was at its height and Homer was singing his songs to the Greeks, the Finns were still living a Stone Age life on the western slopes of the Ural Mountains. Two thousand years later, at the beginning of the Christian Era, these Finns were on the southern shores of the Gulf of Finland. Their eyes were turned north—what strange attraction did the barren Northland mirror before them, blinding from them the visions of the warm South and its golden cities? They built boats, sailed bravely across the gulf and landed on the southern coast of Finland. That strange attraction still drew them northward, and the Finns brushed through the forests and settled on the shores of a glorious lake. Dissatisfied, some of them wandered farther away, to the southern coasts (*Finland Proper*), a few stayed where they were (*Häme*) and the rest moved eastward toward Russia (*Carelia*) to greet the more timid of the Finns who were coming into the same region by land, over the Neva and around the shores of Lake Ladoga.

If St. Henry's fountain had looked about itself at this time it would have found the three tribes dwelling in little scattered communities of log huts, living by hunting and fishing and tilling the soil, looking after their families, going to courts to seek justice. It would have found them hammering iron in their forges, trading weapons and furs and cloth with Novgorod, Byzantium, Bagdad. It would have believed with the Finns that everything in nature had a soul, that the souls of men were immortal; believed their soothsayer and magician priests who knew how to heal the sick and prevent illnesses because they knew the secrets of nature. On long winter evenings it would have heard them singing of their heroes, singing the songs that became their epic. Here was a people with government and commerce, religion, a language and an epic—all the culture that means a nation. It would have seen this nation suffering frequent invasions by the destructive Vikings until they learned that skill themselves and promptly retaliated by invading Sweden, plundering Stockholm and leaving it a field of ashes.

This was too much for the Swedes. Their king Erik had a sense of the dignity of the throne, coupled with the bourgeoisie blood of his father which probably gave him a certain sense of morality, so he determined to go on a Crusade to Finland. Hadrian IV, who had visited Sweden in person a couple of years earlier, gave his blessing. Archbishop Henry of Upsala (who was English, some claim Scotch) came along to do the Christianizing. Soon the little spring on the hill above Turku was disturbed, its sparkling purity desecrated by the blood of those who were unwilling to see the benefits of baptism. It was by all counts a successful crusade: the Finns made Henry their patron saint, and Erik became St. Erik to the grateful Swedes because he had overcome those Finns who had dared to learn a lesson and pillage their neighbor. . . .

Erik laid the cornerstone for a castle and went back to Sweden, but Henry stayed on to build a church. He called the trading place of the Finns

14

Turku, and the city flourished in its barter with Novgorod, Byzantium and Bagdad.

Today the church is Turku's pride, and ships dock in the shadow of Turku's castle. White boats unload tourists; dirty tramp steamers look for cargoes of cellulose and matches, bobbins and sweet-smelling lumber. But the streets, proud with their burden of rattling trucks and automobiles, streets bordered with modern buildings designed to be purely functional and materialistic—these streets are meek and do not dare to go beyond the castle where men have fought and the cathedral where men have prayed.

I do not remember Turku in great detail. It is a dull city. There was nothing out of the ordinary in bourgeoisie Turku, a city sleeping in the summer sun, waiting for the autumn when the students would again gaily throng its streets and cafés. There were no experiences which could recall Turku clearly enough to make me write of it with glowing enthusiasm. It is a city where one feels it is always yesterday.

It is not altogether my fault that I remember such trivialities as being amused by the Englishman who took voluminous notes in the castle, or smiling at the Finnish girl who tried to explain life in Finland to her American guests. I remember that there is a shop selling chromium furniture almost in the shadow of the Gothic cathedral, that the library is baroque, that the museum is full of depressing paintings which look as if they were the result of a three-day storm, a gloomy winter, or a year of poor harvests. Turku seemed dead, its vitality captured in the stones of the castle and the cathedral. I remember that in an antique shop I found an old pewter plate and a picture of the cathedral, that I bought a ticket to Antwerp and a tweed jacket, now left at home because the cuffs are a little frayed.

I was completely alone in Turku; I talked with nobody but the hotelkeeper's buxom, good-natured wife. I was disturbed by a nostalgia, torturing but pleasant, which I did not try to break: a mood where nothing in life seemed of any sense or value. I was homesick, alone, and longed to be in one of those other places where I had not been alone, places where I had been too fascinated to think of anything but the immediate moment. Perhaps Turku reminded me too much of home, just as Stuttgart had once done: standing on the hill-top, seeing the lights of the city glowing in the valley and on the other hillsides.

I have not seen Turku again. Last summer I planned to visit it and was even ready to go one day, but then I got a telegram from my Aunt Mimi. She was in Tampere and wanted to see me. Mimi's invitations are more commands than suggestions, so I

16

took the next train for Tampere, deciding that I could see Turku some other time. But I never thought of it again, and now the battered pewter plate, the old print of the cathedral and a jacket with frayed cuffs are all that remind me of the cradle of Finnish civilization.

Back in Rauma, a critical aunt looked over my purchases. She was contemptuous of the battered old plate, for surely I could have bought a new one for the same money. As for the jacket, she herself preferred English cloth. Then she was silent—she saw the ticket to Antwerp and did not want me to leave. "But first you must go to Kokemäki to visit your cousins!"

I went, but it was only afterward in America that I learned from my father that in Kokemäki the wooden hut where St. Henry preached is still standing, that it was near Kokemäki where Henry met his death one winter night.

A martyr's death is not a pleasant one, and I dare say Henry would have wished it otherwise. On one of his long trips through the countryside, preaching to the peasants and converting them, Henry approached a manor-house late in the afternoon of a day in January, when the ice on the rivers and lakes was at its thickest and the snow on the ground at its deepest.

"It is Lalli's estate!" a servant rode up in chagrin. "We have just met one of his serfs."

"Lalli's?" The bishop was dismayed. "But it is late," he added thoughtfully, "and we are hungry. We must go there anyway—surely they will not refuse us food."

The servant bowed and rode ahead to the manor, a fortress-like place perched on an upland, surrounded by the huts of the serfs in the valley below.

"Is the master here?" asked the bishop as he walked into the hall and was met by Lalli's wife. "No? Then I must ask you for food for my men. We have come far and are hungry."

The mistress Gertrude hesitated. "No—I cannot give you food," she replied curtly. It was what Lalli would have said had he been there.

The bishop flushed from anger and commanded his men to take whatever they needed. Then he walked up and carelessly threw three gold pieces on the table: "For the food," he said, made a sign to his men, turned abruptly about and left. The company slowly descended the hill and went on its way.

Lalli came home from the forest soon afterward and heard about the bishop's visit. Lalli was furious. Perhaps no one in Finland hated the new religion and hence the bishop as much as Lalli. He walked back and forth impatiently while his horse was being saddled. Now he rode as fast as his stallion could carry him along the tracks in the snow. Lalli sighted the party about eight miles away, and by the icy shores of Lake Köyliö he reached the bishop and killed him with one mighty blow of his battle-ax.

"Affront me, the Lord of Köyliö? No, no, foolish bishop, never!" Lalli laughed loud and long. He set the so foully murdered bishop's miter on his own head and rode gleefully homeward.

"But Lalli, where did you get such a splendid crown?" Gertrude asked her husband on his return.

"It is the bishop's." Lalli began to take it off in order to look at it himself. The hat was on tight; it would not come off. Lalli was impatient and pulled harder.

"Your hair!" cried his wife in amazement.

The miter was off at last—and with it, all of Lalli's raven-black hair.

For centuries this story of Henry's death has been told and repeated and embroidered, but even more miraculous than the story of Lalli's losing his raven-black locks, and believed by all good Christians of the Middle Ages, was the legend of the jeweled ring which the bishop always wore on his thumb. Lalli wanted the ring and cut off the thumb in order to get it, but it fell from his greedy hands and was lost in the soft snow covering the ice of Lake Köyliö. It was dark, and though Lalli searched long for the ring, he could not find it.

FINLAND

Early that same spring a blind old man was being rowed across the lake by his young son. The old man, used to listening carefully because he could not see, first heard a noise. "Son, what is it I hear? Do you see it? What is it?" he asked.

The boy rowed on. In the distance he saw a block of ice floating on the water. "It is a block of ice, Father, the last on the lake—and Father, there is a raven crowing on the ice, pecking at something!" He began to row faster in that direction. "Father—it looks like a man's thumb with a ring on it!" cried the lad.

"A thumb with a ring? Quick—it is Bishop Henry's —give it to me!" The boy gave him the thumb, and the old man piously rubbed his eyes with it and exclaimed, "I can see! I can see! I can see!"

And ever since that time a thumb with a ring has been a part of the great seal of Turku cathedral.

Lalli was typical of those who most resisted Bishop Henry and his new faith. "I receive the new religion?" we can imagine him repeating. "No, never! Never will I give up the gods of the Northland." And after these exclamations of anger at the new belief and the hated bishop who was bringing it in, he would stride away to his little shrine in the forest. "Bishop Henry? Bah, he is a fool!"

Why not? Here were the old pagan forces resisting the new, resisting with typical Finnish stubbornness the change that was forced upon them.

Finnish paganism was not barbaric; it did not require the blood of human beings. It was a shamanistic religion dependent on poets: poets who could sing charms and incantations (which have remained as the foundation of Finnish literature) and through this singing force the elements to the service of man. The pagan Finns believed in a supreme god, Jumala, who created and ruled the earth, surrounded by a circle of lesser gods, some good, others evil.

Jumala had delegated the bringing about of our physical world to his sons Wäinämöinen and Ilmarinen, the heroes of the epic *Kalevala*. Ilmarinen was the god of the air; Wäinämöinen formed the earth, formed it through song, brought life to it, and growth. The lesser gods ranged from the gods of the sea, the sun and the moon to Tuoni, who ruled in the land of the dead. And death—was it so terrible? One lived after death, in a land to be sure bleaker than before, in a land where the sparkling blue of the sky and the water and the green of the forest became a duller, cloudier hue. But one lived.

These gods personified in the *Kalevala* actually lived in the spirit of the people, who felt them everywhere in nature. The Finnish place of worship, therefore, was no church of four walls and a roof but a sacred grove, a spring, a tree. How could the priests of a religion like this be anything but poets? Theirs was the task of singing away evil, of healing, of seeking the help of the gods. Even Wäinämöinen, personified as an earthly hero, did not rely on the sword but fought his battles with songs, and today, if you look at the monuments in the public squares, you will not find soldiers in bronze, not palm-waving angels of peace with judicious fig-leaves and discreet draperies, but memorials to poets.

Then came Christianity, pressed on the people not because they were pagans but because these pagans had sacked Stockholm and left it in ashes. Henry became a saint, and his thumb and ring assumed healing powers. The groves, the springs, the sacred trees where people had gone to pray were deserted—people had to worship God in a gloomy stone church that was at the same time a fortress, because somehow a fortress was now imperative to peaceful worship. Later, when the Swedes decided that Luther and not Rome was right, the Finns, too, became Lutherans, and the fortress churches, which had received gay murals in red and blue and green, were whitewashed and became bleak and gray again. . . .

"That is too rational for me," declares Heine's Herr Hyacinth: "And if the Protestant churches did not have organs, there would be no religion at all. Confidentially, this religion is as pure as a glass of water. . . ."

Confidentially, in Finland the organ plays only a small part, and the sermon is the thing. A Finnish sermon is as interminably long as a Finnish train ride. One day in northern Finland, on just such a train ride, a strange silent group came into the carriage where I was sitting and thinking in dismay of the vastness of Finland and the slowness of the trains. In came a wrinkled old woman, looking hard and indignant. She limped along the aisle, then turned back to see if the others were not following: an unshaven, powerful-looking man in a plaid shirt, muttering a sharp *"Tule!* Come along!" to a sullen youth. When they passed me, I looked closer at the boy: his hands were tied behind his back with heavy leather thongs.

The lad might have been a criminal. Perhaps he was an orphan who had run away from the nagging, wrinkled old woman. He might have stolen a pound of sugar from her, or even slept with her daughter. I don't know. In any event the Reverend Thomas Smith would have approved the sight of the boy being brought to justice. You see, in 1815 the Reverend Mr. Smith published his *Repository of Useful and Polite Literature: Comprising Geography, Mythology, Ancient History.* Looking at Sweden, the Reverend related "as an instance of the equity and laudable attention of Swedish magistrates" the following tale "peculiarly deserving" the attention of his readers:

"At Turku, in Finland, a dog which had been accidentally run over by a carriage, crawled to the door of a tanner; but the man's son, a youth of fifteen years of age, instead of pitying the wretched animal, first stoned it, and then deliberately poured a vessel of boiling water upon its body. This abominable act of cruelty was seen by one of the magistrates, who represented the matter so strongly to his brethren, that they unanimously agreed to make an example of the offender. Accordingly he was imprisoned until the following market day, when he was led to the place of execution by an officer of justice, and the following sentence was read to him in the presence of a multitude of people:

" 'Inhuman young man! because you did not assist the animal that implored your aid by its cries, and which derived its existence from the same God who gave you life;—because you increased the tortures of the agonizing beast, and murdered it; the council of this city have sentenced you to wear on your breast the name you deserve, and to receive fifty stripes.' He then suspended a black board from his neck with this inscription: *A savage and inhuman young man!* and after inflicting upon him twenty-five severe stripes, he proceeded: 'Inhuman young man! you have now felt a very small portion of the pain with which you tortured a helpless animal in its dying moments. As you wish for mercy from that God who created all living beings, learn humanity for the future.' He then executed the remainder of the sentence."

Such was eighteenth-century Christian Turku. Naturally there was another side to it, too. For instance, there was the Turku that Salome saw—not that later Lou Salome who exchanged Finland for Italy and almost captured Nietzsche's heart in the process, but the Rubenesque Salome, powerful-limbed, beautiful and intelligent, produced by the imagination of the eighteenth-century German author who wrote romantic novels of improbable adventures such as young Goethe's more frivolous friends might have read.

Salome was so beautiful that barons and dukes fought for her hand, so curious that she experimented with herbs the very breath of which was enough to kill, so learned that at fourteen she presented a thesis *de vera castitate* at the university. What a university! The author had probably looked at Heidelberg and given its pattern to Turku, making it a university of three thousand students, including three Russian princes and two princes from Holstein, miscellaneous aristocrats from most of Europe, plus a bourgeoisie element added to by Armenians,

25

FINLAND

Chinese and Jews! As a result the university was not exactly peaceful, what with national jealousies, intrigues and, no doubt, the presence of Salome. In reality Turku was never as large, cosmopolitan and turbulent as that. The closest the university got to any excitement in the eighteenth century was during those two or three periods when Russia threatened Finland and the professors picked up their academic robes, hopped over the puddles in the muddy lanes, and scampered off to Sweden for safety. I do not know if the students' reactions to these flights have been recorded in not too virtuous Latin, but the exodus threatened to become customary until the Russians put a stop to it by finally capturing Turku, the intellectual center of Finland.

The intellectual center it certainly was. After Henry's followers had Christianity running more smoothly, and the churches became less fortress-like and more gay with their murals in red and blue and green, the bishops turned their attention to still more wordly matters, to the production of such things as new hymns, punishments for those people who refused to go to church on Sundays, a Finnish Bible, and illegitimate children. The bishops also decided, about the beginning of the seventeenth century, when they had parted with Rome and covered the murals with whitewash, that their sheep who could not read the Catechism would be denied the right to marry. That was the end of illiteracy in Finland once and for all, for even their pagan proverb had declared that one regrets everything but marrying when young.

Three centuries ago the Renaissance reached Finland: in 1640, four years after the founding of Harvard, Turku got its university. It was the creation of Per Brahe, that energetic governor whom Queen Christina had sent to rule Finland. An excellent job he did of it, too. For three years he traveled every corner of Finland, strengthened castles, founded cities, built castles, gave cities trading rights, moved cities, and sent glowing reports back to preoccupied Christina: "On the whole this land is so big and in ways so rich—especially the catches of fish, not only from the ocean but also from its numerous big lakes, exceed those of all known lands; there is plenty of decent forest, full of birds and fur-bearing animals; minerals are being found—that, if God grants it to reach that condition which an able imagination sees possible, then in my opinion it should be compared (not on account of its huge size) to some, and not the smallest, European kingdoms."

Per Brahe was the first who actually saw the possibilities and who had imagination enough to rule on a large scale. The petty, meticulous and oppressing rule of the former governors had simply impoverished the land, for the people became lazy and their passion was not for work but for liquor. Brahe brought in a new spirit, and the founding of a university became an integral part of it, the deed the Finns best remember and revere him for. So the university (with eleven professors and forty-four students) opened its doors with an elaborate celebration. It was a lovely July day. The whole city was festooned with flowers, the river full of boats flying flags and pennants. At seven in the morning Brahe stepped out of the castle, headed a long procession, made a speech and attended a service at the cathedral. There was music and laughter, cheering and waving of flags, the blowing of trumpets and the firing of cannon. Eleven proud professors and forty-four bewildered students.

The chronicles do not make clear whether this shouting and cheering and bombs-bursting-in-air were all because a university had been founded or whether it was because Per Brahe left Turku that same day to go home to Sweden.

At any rate the university prospered, and the old city of Turku had one more reason for pride, though not much reason for pride of accomplishment. The hundred and fifty years that followed were more or less sterile intellectually. There were wars to be fought—one after the other. It seemed a question simply of what nature Finland's death was to be— complete destruction by the Russians, or equally complete loss of feeling of Finnish nationalism at the hands of the Swedes. The pagan, Finnish nationalism had disintegrated under the onslaught of Christianity to a point where there was no feeling of nationalism—neither awareness of the old, nor desire to go along with Sweden. A few *Fennophiles* tried to combat the latter possibility. One of them, Daniel Juslenius, more enthusiastic but less scientific than the rest, praised Finland and the Finns to the very heavens. According to him, Turku was founded immediately after the Flood, the Finnish soldiers were superhumanly heroic and able, every Finn was born with the gift of poetry on his tongue. (Poetry? A Turku publisher of the time offered a list of forty-eight books: five hymnals, forty religious works, an outline of Swedish law, a useful manual on the diseases of animals, and a book of moral anecdotes.)

According to a more reliable Russian authority, Turku at that time had eighty-five hundred inhabitants, one hundred two streets and alleys, eleven hundred buildings including fifty stone ones of four stories, a police force of thirty-five soldiers and one officer, a fire department with three pieces of hose, a hospital, two dockyards, one factory each for tobacco, sugar and liquor—and nineteen ships called in the harbor within one year.

A few years after Juslenius came Porthan, who gave impetus to the collection of old Finnish poetry, for, in spite of its mixture of pagan sorcery and Catholic mysticism, he declared, it nevertheless showed a few uplifting thoughts in the midst of such nonsense. Porthan also founded Finland's first newspapers. He urged the Finns to be Finnish; he began scholarly studies of Finnish history, language, mythology. Porthan brought forth the roots of a strong Finnish patriotism and nationalism. It was derived partly from the romanticism of the period, but it also fostered that romanticism. A cycle was ended, and a new feeling of Finnish nationalism was kindled. The people began more and more to look upon themselves as Finns.

"We are not Swedes," one of them declared in a statement that became a slogan, "we do not want to become Russians, so we must be Finns."

In the Eighteen twenties three students at the university took the statement to heart. Runeberg—a tall thin youth, slightly stooped, who wore a serious look and his father's yellow overcoat and became the poet of Finnish nationalism. Lönnrot—small, thin, and very poor, the son of a tailor—who became a doctor and spent his life collecting and putting together the ancient *Kalevala*. Snellman—the sharp-faced lad who became a philosopher and statesman, the important awakener of the Finnish spirit.

The three succeeded eminently. They were the three great men the university produced before it fell on evil days. For in 1809 Finland became a grand duchy of Russia, and there followed a century of more autocratically thorough rule than the Finns had ever known. Turku was doomed. The Russians made Helsinki the capital of Finland because it had a better harbor—a harbor, furthermore, that was not quite so close to Sweden or its influence. In 1827 came the fire, and Turku's doom was sealed. One evening a milkmaid had gone to clean her master's barn: an hour later the building was aflame, another hour and all Turku was burning. The fire swept the city from one end to the other, from the castle to the cathedral. The university and its library burned to ashes. For a week the city was a mass of glowing embers. The Russians shrugged their shoulders: the university moved to Helsinki and promptly became the Royal Alexander University.

Turku swept up the ashes, felt content that it still had its cathedral and castle, and went calmly to sleep.

The cathedral did not come out of the fire unscathed. Parts of it were badly burned; treasures were lost; the caskets in the tombs rose up with the heat and the crumbling stone and fell back in disorder, a mass of shattered wood, brittle bones and dusty velvet shrouds. A generation of vandals did the rest. But now the restored cathedral stands serene once more; venerable, distinguished, carrying its seven hundred years with timeless dignity. Even the clock in the tower (just as in some New England meetinghouse) does not bother itself too closely with mere minutes.

I was interested in minutes, for the day was hot, and the long dull walk along the river, a tortured blue mass between hot stone embankments, had made it seem hotter still. Long rows of tiresome buildings. A lonely tree, the leaves rustling expectantly, eager for a breeze that did not come. No place for a cool drink. I was in no mood for a cathedral. I swore. Had the damned building retreated? hadn't I walked far enough? A little bend in the river, with the embankment unwilling to give way too much; a row of trees throwing their shade over the edge to frame the reflection of a tower in the water. There it was: a massive building in gray and dull red, cool and unmoved. A simple building, almost brusquely so. A few small windows, a few scars of the eternal battle against centuries of weather, fire and besieging armies. No flying buttresses, no lacy carving; no writhing figures, no monstrous gargoyles. No nuns, no priests; no sightseeing busses, no souvenirs. No pigeons. . . . Simply a massive, unadorned building, with a band of cool green trees around it. Sanctuary.

Inside, a refreshing coolness. Not the dark deceptive coolness of more southern churches where the cold creeps slowly out from the depths, where the cold air slowly stifles the throat with a mixture of dampness and hovering incense. Here all is spaciousness, height, a frank coolness from the stone floor and the white walls soaring upward to be knotted together at the top with simple, forceful vaulting. Details of red brick against the white walls, with here and there fragments of faded medieval frescoes in blue and green and red. Rows of chapels, with the tombs of warriors who had fought for Finland and their king on the battlefields of Breitenfeld, Pultava, the Neva; of the wives they left at home; of Queen Karin who had been ill-at-ease on the throne and unhappy when she left it; of bishops who had been weak and bishops who had been strong. The strong ones increased the glory of their church and the wealth of their cathedral—but whatever gold they added has long since been torn away by marauders; the cloud of incense in which they walked has long since ceased to haunt the cathedral whose walls have cast mystery aside, to stand cool and white and frank, serenely soaring toward heaven. The weak ones lived in their fortress in the firs, surrounded by soldiers and flattering followers—but for centuries that castle has been a ruin, a bit of wall standing here, a mass of stone there.

Tall granite cliffs rise up along the sea. The sea rushes angrily at the rocks, and inch by inch they slowly crumble away and reveal the land behind them: the fertile land where gnarled oak trees grow,

FINLAND

the green-growing land where apple and cherry and pear ripen in the warm sun, where towns crowd against towns and countless church spires lift themselves up into the skies.

Here, on the edge of the sea, on the border of a deep forest of firs, rose the castle of the bishops now a mass of ruins and blocks of stone which once were walls that no arrow could pierce, turrets which no enemy could climb. In this fortress in the firs there had been much wealth: gold and silver and splendid jewels locked and hidden in the vaults, the sound of happy voices lost in the cold gray rock.

Here the bishop led a merry life, and his guests were always entertained with music and wine and gaiety. But these times soon came to an end—fire, then invaders, finally Gustav Vasa ordering the building torn down. Not long after that, he ordered some of the blocks of granite to be used in the building of a church in the neighboring town. Soon even the peasants came and carted away block after block for their sturdy stone barns.

Many years after that, the legend relates, came a time when crops were poor and food was scarce. The peasants could not buy any grain, for they had no money. One poor man, Matthew by name, more daring than the rest, went to his wealthy neighbor to ask for a loan of barley for seed. And though his barns were full to the roof-timbers, the Squire was arrogant: he would lend no one a single grain.

"Let them all starve," he said to his steward. "It is their own fault."

Matthew went homeward with his empty sack and sat mournfully among the ruins of the fortress in the firs. Was he to face another year and certain starvation? If he had seed to plant, surely he would get a good crop. If only he had a little barley. . . .

Suddenly Matthew heard a rustling sound behind him. He turned around and saw a stream of grain slowly trickling from a crevice in the wall.

Matthew quickly filled his sack, and when the plowed fields were rich and brown and moist in the warm spring sun, he sowed his seed.

It can only be fate that gave Matthew a rich harvest and the Squire a crop all spoiled. "First of all the frost," the Squire explained to his neighbors, "and then my land was too wet all summer. . . ."

It is one of those few legends (like that of St. Elizabeth of the Wartburg) where the romance of a castle is more than faint music, the rustling of silk, and buried jewels. It is strange that the Wartburg should have been so cruel to one like Elizabeth and have welcomed Luther warmly a few centuries later, for Luther is indirectly responsible for the fortress in the firs being nothing more than a pile of stone and a legend: it was sacrificed when the church accepted the Reformation.

The reform was peaceful on the whole. Bishops still ruled from Turku: they simply put aside their incense and colored robes, covered the frescoes with whitewash, and listened in awe to the teachings from Wittenberg. One eager young student, Michael Agricola, went to Wittenberg, sat at the feet of Luther and Melanchthon, and returned to Turku to become a bishop and the father of Finnish literature.

Agricola's talent was not a creative one. Calm and stolid, traits he had inherited from his fisherman father, he went to school in Viipuri and Turku. Pious, he listened eagerly to the teachings of Luther, became the bishop's secretary, and bemoaned the fact that the people of Häme and Carelia had pagan gods in their memory and were thus led to destruction by the devil and their own sinfulness. Patient, he wanted to save as many of them as possible. Urged by Luther's example, he began to translate the New Testament into Finnish, but realizing the people would have to know how to read first, he wrote and published his *ABC*, the first Finnish book. Then followed prayer books and manuals, psalms and hymn books in rapid succession, and finally, crowning his work, the New Testament. Strange that while the people of Häme and Carelia still had the ancient Finnish songs on their tongue, and sang the epic that was their heritage, the first Finnish book had to be an *ABC*. . . .

It was a new spirit, a new age. Wittenberg was serious, salvation-bent, not the same as the gay Paris where Magnus Tavast had sent his son a century earlier. Magnus was perhaps the most splendid, the mightiest of the Finnish bishops. A Finnish aristocrat and an able statesman, he was both pious and worldly, loved and hated. Everyone bowed to this fifteenth-century bishop as if he were "some royal majesty." Under him the church became more powerful; there was more wealth, more ceremony. The state, too, became better organized, for through his friendship with the king Magnus was able to establish new courts, set up schools and hospitals, establish a monastery, and even a mint. (Once his king refused Magnus' advice: there followed a revolt, banishment—and the king spent the rest of his days as a pirate.) In spite of all his hustling, he had time to devote to his illegitimate son, Olav, whom he educated in Turku and then sent to Paris. Olav had inherited his father's gifts and advanced rapidly. At the Sorbonne he was always first in street fights and was soon elected rector of the university. He hurried home to tell father the good news and was promptly given a parish. Olav took over the income but not the responsibility and dashed back to Paris.

FINLAND

He was again elected rector, and in this capacity he had to give his opinion on whether Jeanne d'Arc should be executed or not. His opinion on the matter has been lost, but when he went home again, he was given still greater honors. After this he went on a visit to Rome, returned home and remained there to become bishop when his father Magnus retired to Naantali, *Vallis gratiae,* to the monastery he had founded in the name of St. Birgitta.

Birgitta was an unusual woman: in the Finnish statues of her she is always seated like the Madonna, wearing that alternately careworn and benign smile that might be Mary's, but in her lap she has not a child but a book. Possibly this learned aspect made the Finns think this Swedish lady did not busy herself with household tasks as a woman should. At any rate, an old Finnish poem relates that Birgitta was tired of spinning and threw the distaff of wool into the river. It bobbed up and down on the waves, and a gust of wind brought it to a tree-lined shore. The Virgin Mary went to see what it was, found the wool —and from that was born the bear that roams the Finnish forests.

When Birgitta's husband died she entered a convent, had some visions and founded her own monastery: a monastery for both monks and nuns, under the leadership of an abbess. The nuns were to do embroidery and help the poor, the monks were to preach and care for the souls. Birgitta went to Rome to get the Pope's blessing for her order, but when she found Urban V in Avignon, she convinced him he should return to Rome. He did. He did not stay long, but Birgitta stayed there for the rest of her life.

The monastery in Naantali grew in wealth and prestige to become Finland's most important. The nuns made lace and stockings, the monks preached, just as Birgitta had planned. In the evenings the nuns walked two by two into the gray stone church on the hill, and the monks sat with the travel-weary pilgrims in the town below, chatting over a glass of *Kirschetrank*. A mere century later this life came to an end. The monastery closed its doors, the monks scattered to become country priests, and St. Birgitta became again a wooden figure who had cast aside her distaff and held an open book in her lap.

In the centuries that followed the decay of the monastery, this vale of grace remained a busy agricultural town, with windmills dotting the hillside and pouring out sack after sack of grain. During this period a gay young blade (had he had too much *Kirschetrank?*) fired his musket at some crows on the church roof—the roof caught fire and half burned the church. But one heritage remained: the nuns had taught the inhabitants of the town clustered around the cloister how to knit stockings. Women and children knit stockings, their husbands knit stockings—even the burgomaster and the town council knit stockings. Twenty-six thousand pair a year. (My father comes from Rauma, a city older than Naantali. "The men knit stockings, the women sift ashes in Naantali," said the complacent burghers of Rauma when this industry flourished.)

Then a warm spring was found, later healing clay, and Naantali became a resort for the ladies and gentlemen of Turku. A resort, but what an idyllic one.

Like a town on the Rhine. A gentle wooded hill rolling down to the shore, incredibly blue water, a long row of islands sheltering the city and making the sea look like a gentle river. Narrow lanes, crowded houses, and every time the eye looks up—the gray spire of the church framed in trees, rising above the warm red houses, the rowan trees and the oaks. ("Why, it shines like the sun in Naantali," the disgusted burghers of Rauma would say after they heard Naantali's boasts.) Eight hundred people—the inhabitants of this smallest of the Finnish cities do not seem eager to move away from their quiet corner, their vale of grace.

What could be finer than to swim in that invigorating blue, eat a leisurely meal, take a glass of mineral water and then a walk to forget its taste; poking along the lanes that seem to have no pattern besides their own willfulness to end up where they please; appraising the plums, cherries, and apples ripening in the neighbor's garden; admiring the shade of his oak tree and the curve of the rowan tree in his garden; smiling at the angles of the houses that would shock any decent carpenter. (In Rauma they used to say: "There are two streets in Naantali: the pigs walk on one when it rains, the burghers on the other when it shines.") Then, in the evening, sitting in the churchyard, a real *Paradiesgärtlein;* trying to read with the sun hovering low to give everything a fantastic glow; at dusk listening to the vespers from the church tower. (The Rauma burgher would yawn and say to his wife: "I have to go to Naantali to buy time.") A life away from the rush of the world, aside from the near-by city of Turku with its hot pavements and docks and steamers pouring out smoke in front of the castle.

Perhaps more than one war lord gazed out of the tiny windows high up in the tower of the castle, over the forests and meadows, and thought of the vale of grace; he shrugged his shoulders with a sigh and went on with his business of ruling Finland from a castle in the middle of a meadow. Strange that there should be nothing castlelike about this setting—no formal gardens, no impregnable cliffs, no miles of primeval forest, no stormy sea. Simply a lush green meadow. Massive rosy gray walls rise high over the poplars and the maples. Square and prosaic, perhaps at first you might mistake this castle for a grain elevator, or think it a prison. Inside, a hushed atmosphere trails you as you begin a pilgrimage through centuries and walk through endless regal suites that are lifeless museum pieces. Stifle the yawn. Is the panorama of the centuries to be summed up in what so many castles offer as their *coup de grâce:* "Napoleon slept in this bed . . .?" Does the spirit of the bygone ages rest only in portraits on the walls and in collections of swords? In chairs and cupboards?

All turbulence is gone. The tourist walks meekly, a bit awe-inspired, a bit bored. His feet echo a dull thud. Not even the slamming of a door is heard. There is no food in the kitchens, no stamping of horses in the courtyard, no laughter from a dark corner.

Yet, here it is, this castle. It has seen times of regal magnificence and lean times when it has served as a prison or merely a storehouse for grain and gunpowder. And during those troublous times when Swedish lords deposed their kings with startling frequency and struggled to be kings themselves, Finland was one of their richest prizes. The castle of Turku was key to the land, but it was not always easily won. Least of all when the mighty Claus Fleming was governor. Duke Charles found that out. Even when a chance bullet had killed the mighty Fleming almost in the arms of his wife, the task was not ended. Madame Ebba was as brave as her husband and firmly withstood the siege. Perhaps Duke Charles would never have become king if a traitor in the castle had not turned men's heads—they filled the cannon with sand and then fled into Charles' hands. There was nothing to do but give up, but even then Duke Charles did not believe that Claus Fleming was dead, did not believe perhaps that a woman could have been so brave. He demanded to see Fleming's body, looked at it, tweaked the man's beard and snarled, "If you were alive now, that head of yours would not rest so safe."

"Sire," the courageous Ebba retorted, "if he were alive Your Highness certainly would not be here now."

Here lived Duke Johan and his bride, until his brother Erik ousted them. And a few years later Johan was king and Erik himself was prisoner here, high up in a tower room. He could look down from the barred window and see the hut at the edge of the meadow where his queen stayed that she might be close to him. Karin was a devoted wife. She had been unhappy as queen, and now surely she was hardly more fortunate. Karin's and Erik's became tragic lives that poets might have the slender threads to weave their songs of love and romance.

Finland's only queen. . . A peasant girl, the daughter of a soldier. It was when she was selling fruit at the market-place in Stockholm that Erik met her, or perhaps he saw her when she was a waitress in a restaurant. An attractive girl, blue eyes, round rosy cheeks, a short stub nose, and a gentle smile on her lips. Good-natured, of course. And Erik, whose hand had been refused by Elizabeth of England and Mary of Scotland, whose eccentricities amused the nobility and angered his brother, defiantly brought Karin into his castle, educated her, and married her when she was old enough, with their son Gustaf in his mother's arms and the little Sigrid walking along with her father.

The court was horrified. One courtier presented the king a magnificent robe, of the finest cloth, with a patch of homespun on the back; Erik returned the gift with the patch covered with jewels. Homespun she was, this Karin, but worth the jewels for her devotion. She had exchanged the simple peasant life and its security for a life that baffled her, left her puzzled, bewildered in all but her steadfast love for Erik. Duke Johan cruelly strove for the upper hand, and finally Erik was a prisoner in the tower room of Turku castle, and Karin lived patiently in a hut at the edge of the meadow that she might be near him, in the hope that she might see him looking out of the window and wave a reassuring hand. Then Erik died, and Karin lived a solitary life on her manor of Liuksiala, a lonely place, with trees and lakes and lapping waves to keep her company. In comparative poverty, for she knew nothing about money and gave too freely to the poor. But happy, too—the lady of the manor, a solid peasant woman in noble dress, in ermine and gold-embroidered velvet, ruffle and jewels—there were practical things to do, the spinning and weaving to look after, her daughter to bring up, and her son to worry about.

Did an unfortunate queen ever have a more unfortunate son than her Prince Gustaf? Duke Johan had commanded that Gustaf should be taken from his mother, put in a sack and drowned. . . . He was smuggled to Austria, where the emperor sent him to school. Soon Gustaf became a beggar, a stable boy, later a bootblack in Vienna. A beggar again, he wandered on foot to Warsaw, saw his sister and pleaded to see his mother. Then awhile as a priest in Posen. After that, a guest of Boris Godunov—but when Boris offered the prince his daughter and was refused, Gustaf was sent to an outlaw regiment and beaten to death. Soon after that Karin died in Liuksiala, a disillusioned tired old woman who had been a queen at the side of the man she loved.

FINLAND

Her body was brought to Turku, a quiet old city that lies between a castle and a cathedral. It is a city where it is always yesterday. The streets are neatly parallel, the river is curbed. And on a hillside over the city a spring flows quietly out of the rock, knowing that today is as yesterday, or yesteryear, or a thousand years.

FRONTIER

VIIPURI IS scarcely younger than Turku. It has no less history, no less significance as a key to Finland. But how vastly different the two cities are, what a contrast they offer! Viipuri is the eastern city, the bulwark at the head of the strip of land that is the gateway to Russia and the east. Turku contented itself with sending stockings to Stockholm, but Viipuri was a brisk Hansa city whose might was known even in Moscow and Flanders. The Russians came every year to buy Finnish horses, because for the Russians no price was too dear for a good Finnish horse. The merchants saw Viipuri flourish and become a prize coveted and contested for by all the Russians from Alexander Nevsky through Ivan the Terrible down to Peter the Great. It is a city which makes Turku seem a dull, out-of-the-way and smug provincial town. Viipuri is exactly opposite: gay, cosmopolitan, a worldly mixture of naïveté and sophistication. It is the unexpected: for centuries a battlefield, it turns out to be a city that bears no scars. It is a compromise of elements that are Finnish and Russian, Swedish and German; it is a paradox, for at one and the same

time it appears the most un-Finnish yet also the
most Finnish of cities.

To go back to Viipuri's origins, we must take a
brief look at ancient Turku. When St. Henry died,
Turku's Christianity fell on lean days. The next
two bishops were mere missionaries, wandering
preachers trying their inspired but feeble best to
keep the new faith alive. One of them was kidnaped
by the pagan Carelians during their invasion of
Finland Proper; his successor was killed when the
Carelians came again, urged by the Russians of Novgorod. In fact, the faith would have been completely
lost during the next generation if the Popes had
not remembered their far-off, untended sheep grazing
perilously close to their ancient sacred groves. The
Popes sent frequent admonitions and bulls to the
Swedish kings, reminding them of their duty. There
were results, eventually. The Swedes sent Bishop
Thomas, an English Dominican friar, into the land.
Stirred by the vision of building a state, Thomas
began work on Turku's cathedral, penetrated successfully into pagan Häme, then plunged into Carelia, determined to wage war against Novgorod,
which was supporting the Carelians in their stubborn paganism. The campaign failed; Alexander
Nevsky smashed the bishop's army. Thomas was so
disappointed he gave up his task and went back to

Sweden. The Carelians in gratitude became Greek Orthodox, and Alexander became a saint.

The raids on Turku continued—the Russians had no desire to see Sweden advancing eastward, and the Carelians did not even need an excuse for fighting—until Birger Jarl, the mightiest of the Swedish lords, decided to try his luck in subjugating the Finns. He penetrated into the heart of Häme with such swiftness the warlike Finns were too surprised to gather an army, so they became Christians and Swedish subjects instead. Birger took no chances: he closed the road to further invasion and plundering of Turku by building the castle of Hämeenlinna. After that the Häme Finns reluctantly became better Christians.

In the next crusading wave, the equally mighty lord Torkel sailed with a big fleet to the eastern end of the Gulf of Finland, landed in Carelia, and built the castle of Viipuri. With this move, six hundred years ago, the Carelians, still more reluctantly than their western brethren, became Christians. They prayed to both the Virgin Mary and their pagan hero Wäinämöinen with equal fervor.

Russia continued to battle at the gates of Viipuri for centuries, but it continued to be defeated: *Moscorum busta Viburgum*—Viipuri, the death of the Muscovites, the barrier beyond which the Russian spirit could not penetrate. The defense was difficult at times, and often it seemed that only the miraculous, help from God or the devil, could save the Finns. Like the *Big Bang* of 1495. In that year the Russians arrived with a bigger horde than ever before: sixty thousand men. But Knut Posse, who had studied physics and chemistry at the Sorbonne, was their equal. While the Finns were appealing to St. Henry and the Russians to St. Alexander, Posse calmly climbed to the highest tower of his castle and emptied a bag of feathers. The Russians were bewildered, for as each feather fell into the bay it turned into a battleship. Perhaps vodka was to blame, the Russians laughed, and charged again with their ladders, faggots and two dozen one-foot cannon. This time Posse filled a huge kettle with turtles, snakes, quicksilver, lye and lime. The Finns stuffed their ears with cotton, an old woman threw a cat into the pot and the mess exploded with frightful fury, a flare of light, and a glowing cross in the sky that sent the Russians into immediate flight. When they were back home they added a new line to their litany: "God save us from the Viipuri bang, the merciful Father protect us from Knut Posse. . . ."

("Not far from Viipuri, reports a sixteenth-century German authority, "there is said to be a cave, called the *Bang,* from which, when one throws in living animals, there issues such a frightful crash and

echo that everyone who hears it falls to the earth, pow-
erless and unconscious for a time. And the Finns are
said to have often used this cave to their advantage
against the Muscovites. In order that everybody
shall not approach it, it is nowadays surrounded
and protected by several high walls.")

In 1709 Peter the Great defeated the forces of
Charles XII of Sweden at Pultava, ending the career
of that nation as an important European power,
and the next spring Peter marched over the ice from
Kronstadt to besiege Viipuri. Three months later
the castle fell, after four hundred years of resistance,
and the keys were handed to the Russians on a silver
platter. For three days the victory was celebrated
with parades, the thanking of God, the spraying of
the entire city with holy water, the drinking of
vodka in a thoroughgoing fashion. Viipuri became
Russian.

Viipuri is still dominated by its castle, and the
castle in turn is dominated by its tall tower which
begins as a square block, turns octagonal half-way
up, and ends in a dome. From the top the view of
Viipuri is superb, but it means a climb of two
hundred thirty-nine steps. I was standing at the foot
of the tower when I heard this startling report and
hesitated long enough to smoke a cigarette. When
Peter the Great made the climb, wines and other
cooling drinks were served at intervals on the way

up, but I had to go ahead unaided. The water-surrounded castle lies close to the mainland, a fat breast of rolling mound. The two are connected by a long low bridge which divides the water into a north and south harbor. Remains of an old city wall skirt the shore of the mainland opposite the castle. A few blocks away, in the center of the city, stands the Fat Katherine, a generously round tower which was once a part of the city wall at the further side. Now the tower, so appropriately named, stands solidly at the edge of the bustling market-place. It is a bulwark against modernism, emphatically marking the end of the Torkel promenade and the new city, turning its back on them and throwing a sheltering shadow over the old city that lies on the gentle hill between the tower and the sea. The hill is covered with stone buildings left by the centuries: medieval churches, towers, iron balconies, old houses on steep, narrow, cobblestone streets with romantic names like Black Friars' Street or the Cattle Gate. Rather like Rothenburg-ob-der-Tauber, but Rothenburg has not added anything, not even a piece of plumbing, since the seventeenth century, whereas Viipuri has grown, attached formal, elegant eighteenth-century squares to itself (like the regal *Königsplatz* of some small German duchy), built parks and promenades, turned ramparts and bastions into outdoor theaters and walks, gone through the mad nineteenth-century cycle of Gothic and Renaissance revivals, advanced to purely functional glass and steel structures.

The population is equally colorful. The Germans are still there, still merchants remembering Hansa glories. The Russians are there, remembering bygone splendor, reluctantly selling an icon or samovar, silver or a treasured heirloom now and then to get food. The Finns are there, too—Carelians, small, lithe, dark, with the *Kalevala* in their blood and a zest for living in their veins.

On summer evenings the whole city promenades in the Torkel, to the music of a military band. Very unmilitary melodies like Strauss waltzes and light opera selections form the nostalgic background to this summer twilight. Silent couples. Soldiers. Two girls walk toward an empty bench, just as a young soldier lad sits down. The girls hesitate a moment and sit on the other end. The soldier moves closer. A blonde, hollow-eyed, coughing, walks past, stops at the fountain with a maiden bathed in streams of water. Perhaps she remembers how often she has seen the fountain late at night, when the water no longer splashes over the figure, and the maiden, with hands over breasts, looks coy and silly. There are more soldiers, clicking spurs, officers saluting. Widows in black, young girls in white. Children on swings, swaying with the rhythm of the music. A

long low row of barracks along one side, the avenue
on the other, smart automobiles and once smart
droshkies driving past the shops and cafés. The
promenade has something of the feeling of Baden-
Baden elegance, the gayness of Copenhagen's carefree Tivoli of light and music, the nostalgic mood
of Proust's frieze of girls at Balbec.

The trees and grass come to a sudden end at a
deserted cobblestone square and the round tower,
trim with its whitewashed walls and tracery of ivy.
The Fat Katherine was not always as serene as this.
Certainly not in those medieval days when a row
of heads hung as a warning fringe under the eaves,
after mass executions in the cobblestone square.
Now you can climb to the top story and sit in a
medieval atmosphere; waitresses in medieval cos-
tumes, complete to the ruff, serve leisurely meals to
the slightly off-tune, uninspired playing of Finnish
folk songs.

Wandering on, you can see the castle in the dusk,
looking majestic and impregnable. Near by is a
statue of Torkel, admiring his castle. There used to
be a statue of Peter the Great, victoriously facing
both Torkel and his castle, but twenty years ago
the Finns wrapped it up and sent it to Petrograd, a
pleasant gesture. Turn left into the older part of
the city and there is suddenly a Russian-looking
tower ahead of you, then a high-walled churchyard,

a medieval tower and a solitary tree leaning toward
the narrow street, deserted and gloomy. A turn, and
you are in the eighteenth-century square, lined with
little palaces. The crystal chandeliers in one high
room are lit, and through the big windows you can
see the dancing couples, hear the carefree laughter
and applause and clicking heels, the music of
rumbas and fox-trots filling the square. A little more
and you are suddenly on the bastions. The city lies
sheltered behind you, in front of you the cool breeze,
the sea, and the glowing scarlet and purple sky.
The steamers glide noiselessly on the mirror sea, a
myriad of lights. There are lights along the harbor
front, past the docks and the gas tanks, the huge
granaries and the mills. A couple of drunks curse
and fight in the street. A hazy smoke pours from
tramp steamers at rest. With grinding noise the der-
ricks unload coal from a steamer into waiting trains,
pushing and jangling. Stevedores are at work, grimy,
soot-covered, hardly hearing the faint strains of
rumbas and fox-trots, the waltzes lilting from the
Torkel, hardly sensing the elegance, the ease, the
gaiety of Viipuri.

The following evening I was near the same place,
at the outdoor theater built among the ramparts.
The stage is a narrow grass plot in front of a high
curved stone wall, from the top of which cannon
used to command the sea. It is a marvelous theater,

for I could turn away from the actors to see the city at my left and the ocean at my right casting their spell over me.

A stout, middle-aged lady (the Fat Katherine come to life) took her place next to me. Almost as soon as she sat down she began to talk, cheerful chatter about the evening, the actors, and there goes the conductor, that man with the violin. She did not mind my turning to my book but interrupted again and again. She explained the action, offered me chocolate. During the play she laughed and chuckled, turned to see if I was not amused, too, then laughed again, the talkative, good-natured Carelian enjoying life. (When she got up to go she said "good-by" and patted my hand.)

The play was a Hungarian piece called the *Red Satchel*. Cheerful calls sounded from far-off, the orchestra began to play a czardas, a group of Hungarian youths and maids danced on the rampart, a frieze silhouetted against the sky. Two gay bachelors in a drinking bout. The rich old husband and his beautiful young wife. A regiment of Hussars. Intermission, and a rush of the audience for coffee and cake. During the next act the moon was rising over the cyclorama, a real moon, trailing its glow over the ocean. Lights were flickering in the city. Darker, then lighted flares on the ramparts as the gay young Hussar found his love had become the rich man's wife. A lost satchel, money disappearing, a gypsy fortune-teller. Misunderstandings and a happy ending. A frieze of Hungarian youths and maids running on the ramparts, disappearing, a *fata Morgana* from the Puzta.

The audience enjoyed every moment of it. Of course it was unreal, it was nonsense. Cheerful froth, music and laughter, a moment of mock tenseness, release. "Nothing pleases the Finns more than acting," a friend of mine declared. Not only literally acting or going to the theater—even the small cities have their legitimate theaters, professional companies, state subsidies—but acting, hiding emotions, appearing serene, or dramatizing life, squeezing every bit of emotion out of it, appearing heroic against overwhelming odds. It is not a shamefaced but wholehearted, zestful performance. It is real; a relentless environment makes it more than froth or mock tenseness. Contrast with that this *fata Morgana:* it, too, is more than a mirage; it is a part of the Finnish temperament, a kinship with gay Strauss waltzes sounding from the Torkel, the fiery czardas filling the veins with excitement, the sad Slavic folk songs filling the heart with melancholy and longing.

These same contrasts that form the character and account for the charm of Viipuri come out strongly in Monrepos, the lovely Viipuri park. In a way it could be compared to Kew Gardens, that huge and dull maze, with no end of lanes and paths; trees and shrubs and plants by the millions, all neatly labeled; schoolgirls, nurses with prams, schoolboys, young artists; pagodas and Greek temple effects, plus conveniences hidden with such Victorian delicacy and tact behind masses of shrubbery you can hardly find them. Respectable, just the thing for a not too adventurous Bank Holiday. Yet Monrepos is different, smaller, more natural, more interesting. There are meadows instead of lawns; there are no labels on the plants.

Monrepos began life as an estate, the home of the Russian governors of Viipuri. The entrance is through a Gothic arch of brown-painted wood, rather like that of the summer stamping grounds of a Salvation Army battalion. A winding road leads to the long, low wooden villa of the von Nicolay, stretched out along a ridge like Sans Souci, white and formal, but not quite playful enough for Voltaire. In front of the villa lie meadows, patches of wood, a bay, islands; in a glade, a statue of Wäinämöinen, a harp in his lap; an obelisk on a high rocky crag; the white front of a Greek temple, with a statue of Pan in a niche (actually it is a bust of Jupiter— but Pan is the one who should be there); a little island with a pinkish stucco castle, horribly pseudo-Gothic; a Chinese pagoda.

LAND OF HEROES

It is best to climb the rocky ledge and survey all these things over a cup of coffee on the terrace of a classic tea pavilion. It is more restful. Why Jupiter (or Pan) is here, I do not know, or why Wäinämöinen. The obelisk is a memorial to a couple of princes who fell in the Napoleonic wars. The fantastic pink stucco, turrets and towers affair is a mausoleum. The pagoda is—well, just there, falling rapidly to ruin, its windows shattered, its frescoes on canvas in moldy tatters. But all these incongruities are rising up from Finnish soil, earth and pink granite, trees of pine and spruce, ash and birch, with a background of quiet bay, and behind the bay the vastness of Finland: hundreds of miles of Finnish forest and lake, meadow and tree-lined shore. It is pleasant to reflect on these symbols over a cup of coffee. The obelisk becomes a monument to power, to empire; the pink stucco castle, a Romantic symbol of release to majestic nature, individualism, freedom. Here the obelisk stands on a higher crag, however, denounces such Gothic principles, smiles on the temple and its feeling of serenity, smiles on the pagoda, a whim of Slavic fantasy. Elegant people have walked in this park, talking of poetry, of love, of conquest, but now it is given over to Finnish crowds, to soldiers and maids, solid peasants, Finnish tourists, who find it a pleasant place on Sunday afternoon. A restful place.

FINLAND

Yes, but as I walked past the long low villa and thought of the *Cherry Orchard,* I saw a group of people at their ease on the terrace, facing the obelisk of empire and the pagoda of Slavic fantasy. There was a sign before the garden gate: *Private.* The park is Viipuri's, it is Finnish; but in the villa live the von Nicolay, and I heard the sounds of gay, animated conversation—a conversation in French.

In Helsinki there is nothing Russian besides a Greek church overlooking the harbor. It is an ugly church of glaring red brick and gilt onions, rapidly falling to ruin; it is a discordant touch, but it in no way dominates or even faintly symbolizes the city. Russia seems far away. It seems just as far away as the train rushes eastward, on to Viipuri. And Viipuri is not Russian, but it is a parting of the ways. The train goes on, over the Carelian Isthmus, slowing its pace, on into Soviet Russia and Leningrad. But from Viipuri another train goes east, too. It steams into Sortavala, into the depths of Carelia, into primeval forests and lakes and loneliness. And here, suddenly, mysteriously, one is in old Russia.

The four hours from Viipuri to Sortavala are dull. The countryside is pleasant enough, but by contrast with the gayness of Viipuri, it suddenly seems forlorn, the distances between stations longer; towns appear nowhere, and farms seem to have retreated except for occasional fields. Solitary grandeur, melancholy as a Finnish folk song.

Sortavala is the jumping-off place for Valamo, the Russian monastery on an island in the Ladoga. Further east than Leningrad, Sortavala is nevertheless a purely Finnish city, for three centuries the victim of frequent destruction in the wars between the West and the East. Surrounded by level fields and forests, it is a modern city, a combination of wooden, one-story Finnish provincial architecture, and, because tourists find their way here, super-functional modern hotels, with terraces and balconies, like some resort on the shores of a Swiss lake. It is a school city: you can learn to be anything from a Greek Orthodox priest to a Lutheran deaconess or sexton, a weaver or an organist or a business executive; you can attend what is one of the largest teacher-training schools in all Scandinavia. Here is Carelia, the home of the *Kalevala,* the land of the heroes.

There is nothing Russian in Sortavala, except for a Greek Orthodox church that does not look particularly oriental; nothing to show that two and a half hours away by slow boat is Valamo. Even the steamer that takes us there is not unusual. It is like all Finnish lake steamers: white and graceful. At the same time it is not Finnish because it is slightly dirty. It is equipped with a dirty Finnish flag. It is further equipped with several icons and one monk. Furthermore, it is not punctual, but slips away from the pier a half hour late, to twist and turn past densely-wooded, steep rocky shores until it finds open water. But once the islands are left behind, another island looms up before us, larger than the rest, the island of Valamo and its Russian monastery.

It is a strange experience. It means leaving the Western world that we understand, the cities and peoples and way of life that are familiar and matter-of-fact (with the possible exceptions of economics, Hollywood, and world politics), and suddenly plunging into the mystery of the East; leaving sober, realistic Finland and coming upon blue and green and silver onions gleaming in the bright sun. They loom over the trees long before anything else is in sight, like some far-off, sacred grove of Böcklin's. Then the boat enters a narrow channel. On the left is the little chapel of St. Nicholas, a weird Russian mixture of Gothic and Byzantine, greeting the voyagers who have come safely across the divide. The shore gets steeper, and soon it is sheer; from the top the white cloister smiles at the pilgrims. Valamo is a smiling land: the cuckoo sings here, and the nightingale; cherries and pears and plums hang heavy on the trees; the fir and the pine have given way to oak and maple and poplar.

It seems incredible that bad spirits lived here once, but they did, only moving out when the monks came, and retreated disgruntled to Sortanlahti (the Bay of Evil Spirits) and Impilahti (the Bay of Nymphs). Sergei of Athos put them to rout. This devout monk preached on the shores of Ladoga, but some Lalli-like pagans, simple as they were, unlearned people who could not resist Sergei's logic, insisted they could not believe him until he went to Valamo, one of their sacred places, and proved his wisdom there before the assembled priests. Sergei went, alone, unarmed, into an unknown land—and conquered. That was nine hundred years ago. He lived alone in a cave, but more and more converts joined him, the monk Herman came from Athos, a church was built, and the monastery began its colorful history. It was built, destroyed, deserted, built again. It suffered defeat, rose to glory. During the last century there were as many as two thousand monks at Valamo; now there are less than two hundred, and the monastery faces the fact that once again it seems doomed to be deserted, to die, perhaps forever.

To die? I saw young lads, scarcely more than twelve or fourteen years old, dressed in the black robes and black boots of novices, running gaily down the stairs of the church, laughing and shouting. The church bells ring gaily, ring joyously, like some invitation to a carnival, dispelling all gloom. And the emperors' "cells," the apartments of Alexander I and Alexander II, still furnished as they left them, their portraits still on the walls, seem to be ready and waiting, the whole monastery seems to be waiting like a grief-stricken parent for a prodigal nation to return and worship. Surely there are still people in Russia who have worshiped at Valamo. Do they have any memories of things past, longings, hopes?

Valamo seems to be divided into three parts. First of all, there is the monastery itself. It is not far from the landing-stage, where monks stand waiting for the boat to come in, where tourists stand idly by to see what the new flock of tourists will be like, and where Finnish soldiers stand at guard as at the frontier of one world against another. The cloisters, the churches and monastic cells, the cemetery, the hotel for pilgrims and tourists make the setting for the communal life of the monks, a life of hard work and arduous worship which forms this first world.

The second part consists of the some twenty small chapels scattered casually about the group of Valamo islands, with obviously no other purpose than that there shall be chapels wherever one turns, chapels to house a treasured icon, to honor a saint, or give the pilgrim another opportunity for a prayer. These chapels are for those monks who prefer a smaller brotherhood than that of the cloister community. Here some five or six monks can enjoy a relatively solitary life taking care of a little chapel where they worship, in whose shadow they can eat and sleep.

Still other monks, those of the third category, live in complete isolation as hermits. The hermits hide themselves well; in fact, I did not see any of them. Permission to lead this pleasant life of solitude, sleeping in a cave, praying all day and half the night, is granted only to brothers who have first proved themselves exemplary monks in the community. Surely these hermit monks, willing to devote a lifetime to nothing but prayer, should be either heroes or fools. Or completely embittered lovers.

The chapels are interesting. They range from simple log structures all the way to the Gethsemane chapel on the "Mount of Olives" and the Church of the Resurrection, popularly called *Jerusalem*. "Going to Jerusalem" is one of the more popular diversions at Valamo, listed on the daily sheet of activities at the hotel, along with church services and other guided tours, just as more mundane resorts might list a golf tournament or a Tuesday night dance. And for all the religious implications of such an excursion as going to Jerusalem, it is still a worldly pleasure.

We crowd into a launch, a silent monk takes the wheel, and Ivan, a more talkative young novice, comes around with tickets, then with a map, finally with the conventional colorless statistics of any guided tour. We sail around the Hermit Island, big enough for a half-dozen hermits, with liberal stretches of rocky shore and dense forest to ensure adequate privacy for each, past the John the Baptist Island, getting a glimpse of a chapel through the trees, into a triangular bay with palisade walls. We are at Jerusalem. We eye the chapel suspiciously, stand impatiently in line and crawl on hands and knees into the crypt, a replica of Christ's tomb at Jerusalem.

No one reveals any deep emotion. For a moment each of us fears a tension, perhaps a pious reaction, but when we feel intuitively that none of us are particularly interested, that we are all at best but skeptic believers, we go on to Gethsemane in a much gayer mood. Even Ivan is chatting nonchalantly with a young couple. Gethsemane is another chapel, this time of wood. Then up the steep path of the Mount of Olives, and, pagans that we are, we begin to worship the view, the composition of forest and cliff, water and lurid rosy sky.

Ivan chatted gaily with a blonde woman. The young ladies of the party seemed particularly interested in him: his hair was not stringy, his beard was only a suggestion of fuzz, and he spoke English, German and French fluently. Even Mary, who was

English and old enough to know better, tried her luck. But when I asked Ivan about the young lady who had attracted my attention at the vespers service so much that even Mary had given me a nudge, and declared emphatically a monastery was no place for a love affair. I did not get Ivan's answer until later. At dinner in the dingy restaurant the young lady walked by our table and Mary maliciously suggested I invite her to join us. Not necessary, I replied, because she will be at the three o'clock service in the morning. Mary groaned, and we went out for a walk. . . .

Valamo is beautiful, not because it is exotic, but simply because it is beautiful. There is nothing garish about it. The big white buildings look like sprawling chateaux. The churches are more elaborate, of course, but their green and blue and silver cupolas blend with the sky. The lawns, the tree-lined lanes, the magnificent terrace in front of the cloister seem like the setting of the Heidelberg Schloss overlooking the Neckar. Igumen Damaskin, who built the Valamo that now exists, who brought the monastery to such glory and splendor, must have been a man of great ability and vision.

The old cemetery next to the cloisters is a lovely place. Trees and tangling ivy add to the profusion of Russian crosses, and centuries of lives pass in review. One old slab covers the grave of Magnus

FINLAND

Smek, a Swedish king buried in a Greek Orthodox monastery. 1371, an assault on Russia, a storm on the Ladoga, everything lost except Magnus clinging to a plank—so the legend on the stone reads—Magnus rescued by the monks and carried to the monastery where he was converted, became a hermit, lived for three days and three nights and died, his sins forgiven. Like Tannhäuser. Magnus had sinned because he had broken the peace between the Swedes and the Russians, after a treaty which had been sealed with the kissing of a golden cross. Twice Magnus came, and both times he was defeated. Then the Swedes grew impatient—they blamed Magnus for the defeat, blamed him for the dissension in the country, blamed him for the Black Death. The disgraced Magnus went to Norway to live with his son, but he wanted to return to Russia once more to beg forgiveness for his sins. Then the storm on the Ladoga, and a repentant and forgiven Magnus dies on Valamo. It is a peaceful place to live and die, out of the way of the world—even though it is practically in the jaws of Russia. Here, if one were weary of the world, life could be one of quiet and forgetfulness.

I would not like it, for I do not seek forgetfulness. In the end I would probably be no more exemplary than that monk who had been a Russian prince. The Igumen sent him to Sortavala on business; the monk did the errands, saw a poster for a costume dance—and went to the dance. The belles of Sorta-vala wondered who the handsome man was—so polished, such a marvelous dancer, so clever to come dressed as a monk! But when the time for unmasking came, the monk was nowhere to be seen. Of course I could not enter the monastery, anyway, for I am not a Finnish citizen, and I do not speak Russian.

Furthermore, I would be a revolutionary monk, a heretic. The whole monastery would certainly be upset, because I would insist on bathing. Unheard of, that a Russian (or at least, a Valamo monk) should want to wash himself. The monks looked dirty, smelled dirty. Their long hair and beards were a lusterless, indescribable color. And their cells! One monk who took me in tow showed me through the cells: the most vivid impression is one of stench, just plain stench. Ivan seemed to smile ironically when he noticed his charges feel a bit poorly as they passed through the refectory. But why should Ivan worry? He was there only in summer; in the winter he went to school in Helsinki. A summer monk, just as an American college boy might wash dishes in a summer hotel, and cast longing glances at the young lady guests. They do not take their religion too seriously, these young novices. They come, they get tired of the monotony, they leave. The old monks grow older and die, the young seem to prefer the world. The poor food, the smells, the heavy black robe and heavy boots, the incessant work and prayer are easy to forget.

But not the bells. No one can forget the lilting Valamo bells. Mary and I climbed to the belfry to see this miracle of bell-ringing. A young monk stood there, facing the sun, his profile like that of a Michelangelo, so Mary said. Over us hung a huge bell, to one side hung a double row of small bells. We waited. Our Michelangelo pulled a rope, and the huge bell began to vibrate and hum, slow and majestic, with such force I am sure it could be heard in Viipuri if one half listened. Our ears began to ring, and soon the whole tower seemed to quiver every time the big bell rumbled. It finally came to a slow stop, and the landscape seemed to breathe more freely again. Then Michelangelo stepped up to a little platform, took some wires in his hands and began to play the small bells, pouring out light, high metallic tones, accented by an occasional deeper boom. The whole thing again. Once more. Then a pause and another concert that seemed like a variation on the first theme, while down below the monks were beginning to file into the church of the Transfiguration.

Actually, this glory of Valamo is a double church, one over the other (like the Sainte Chapelle in

Paris or the double chapel in Nürnberg). In a building like this, the lower church is dark and somber, but the upper one is a blaze of light. The Valamo lower church, dedicated to Sergei and Herman, is rich enough in decoration, but little light penetrates into the heavy gloom of gold. The upper church, by contrast, is as gaily golden as those bells calling the monks to worship. What a dazzling profusion of gold, bright paintings, frescoes, jewels, rich oriental rugs—treasure enough to robe a thousand Tartar princesses. What an overflow of saints and angels, cherubim and seraphim!

The service itself is fascinating. The Igumen faces the high altar screen, his back to the worshipers, and reads in a calm, unimpassioned, melodious voice. The congregation stands, and every now and then, at some mysterious phrase, everyone bends in a deep bow, then makes the sign of the cross. Old monks hobble in, greet their friends, bow before a saint or two, and join the worshipers. The reading goes on, for half an hour, three quarters of an hour. A few tourists sit down on the benches at the back, but a monk sternly motions them to stand. (Mary solved the problem of tired feet by taking off her shoes.) The melodious voice goes on—then, suddenly, a choir of deep voices responds behind the screen, responds in a beautiful minor song of a Russian Bach. More reading, and then the choir appears in a stately procession to sing in front of us, then disappears again behind the screen as the reading goes on and the worshipers bow and cross themselves and bow again. It lasts indefinitely, but Mary and I did not leave until a monk waving a censer marched through the church, stopping in front of the shrines and the monks, in front of Mary and me to leave us in a halo of fragrant incense.

I was so delighted with this glorious service I decided to get up and attend the three o'clock liturgy. I had never gotten up at three before, but the bell booms so loud it can be heard half-way to Viipuri—I would have no difficulty in waking up. I looked out of my window at the cupolas gleaming in the moonlight. I examined the icon carefully in my blue cell. I pondered over a long text in Russian which I could not understand. Then I went to bed —but I could not sleep. Something kept biting me. Again and again, until I finally cursed the monks roundly for their dirty faces and greasy hair, the dank smell in the corridor, the poor food, the uselessness of a monastery and frumpery and monks in general. Then I slept. In a stupor. I almost missed the boat for Sortavala.

I explained the whole affair to Mary on the boat.

"It would have been simpler if you had gotten out of bed and killed the menagerie," she declared.

I suppose so. We sat in the sun, and I forgot all about it, except I had to scratch my legs a lot. "I don't mind—Valamo was an experience even without that."

Yes, but why should anyone visit Valamo? It is so obviously not a part of Finland, contributes nothing to Finland but a picturesque, alien touch. It would be far better to visit Valamo after a nice conducted tour of Leningrad, perhaps, just to see another, a vanished Russia. But no matter why you visit it—to seek the picturesque, to appreciate a religion, or in order to sneer at it the more intelligently—you are necessarily impressed. It is a significant experience, however, even on a tour of Finland, in an attempt to understand the Finns. It emphasizes the lack of Russian characteristics in Finland and the Finns, but more than that, it brings out the democratic nature of Finland, reveals that democratic tolerance and honesty which not only allow them to see the justice of permitting this anachronism to exist—an anachronism it must be when the Russians themselves have so thoroughly destroyed the church—but also to go so far as to foster it by liberal financial aid from the state budget.

"So you did not get a chance to see that girl, after all," Mary smiled.

The flag at the stern was still just as dirty, and

sparkling Valamo was getting smaller, a mere dot on the horizon.

"There will be others at Savonlinna," I said, scratching my leg.

Lisa, for instance. She lives in Savonlinna. I remembered Savonlinna with special fondness, for three years ago Lisa and I had had a good time there. Besides Lisa, Savonlinna has a castle which is superb, the best you can find in northern Europe. So Mary went on to Helsinki and I jolted along toward Savonlinna, reading a nonsensical book about three men and a girl who were stranded on a desert island. That was a pretty boring tale, so I talked about Danish dietary research with a well-fed lady from Copenhagen. She assumed I knew quite a bit about it, for the Danes had presented their findings in an international conference in Edinburgh. I knew nothing about it, but the Danish lady went on with determination until I looked at my watch and told her that Punkaharju was almost due.

"Punkaharju! I have heard so much about it—shall we see it from the train?"

I nodded, and just then the conductor came in to inform us that we were getting close to Punkaharju. He was of that school of Finnish conductors who know there are things to see in Finland and who make certain the foreigners on their train will be sure to see them. He spoke with no little pride. Soon the Danish lady and I were popping from one window to another to see the famous Punkaharju, that curling ridge which extends for seven kilometers between two lakes, now a thread between the waters, now broadening out to make space for steep forested slopes, now throwing out a little peninsula, or bending to show a new view, placing a little grove here, an open sweep of water there, with the sole purpose that everything shall be delightful, that it shall be a joy to walk along the ridge, a joy to feel alive. We forgot all about dietary research, about conferences and politics. In fact, for a long time we did not have anything to say.

Then we looked out of the window again when the conductor told us St. Olav's castle was hiding behind a bend. What a majestic castle it is! Rosy gray, massive, with three high round towers, walls and bastions rising from a rocky island. I rushed to the platform, scarcely saying good-by to the Danish lady, impatient because the train did not stop then and there. Over a bridge, into Savonlinna, built on a jagged island, like big green slabs from a jigsaw puzzle set in blue water, with the *Kurpark* and casino at the right across a bay, the town on the left, hemmed in by the market-place on the shore, the park where the white steamers tie up (it is called a harbor), the promenade and the parks.

FINLAND

I did not amble along, trying to look nonchalant, as if I had just been packed in mud and healing waters at the Hydro—I rushed through the streets, across the market-place, straight to the shore, like a courier with an important message to the castellan. I rang the bell stuck on the end of a post. I felt self-conscious: surely everyone in Savonlinna heard the bell: some boys looked up from their game, and a couple of fishermen out in a rowboat probably cursed me for the noise I made. The castle looked deserted, as if a Tristan had died there long ago and the shepherd's pipes were stilled forever. Then an old man appeared and began to row across the sound. First upstream, slowly and laboriously, then swiftly down to my very feet. St. Olav's castle stands in the middle of a sound connecting two lakes; the water rushes by with a swift current. Erik Axelsson Tott knew what he was doing when he built this stronghold:

"Anno Domini 1475 I, Erik Axelsson, knight of Lagnö, built this castle to the glory of God and the protection of the holy Christian faith. And at that time my wife was Elin Gustavsdotter, mistress of Lagmansö."

The castle was built right on the border of what was Sweden and what was Russia, built to strengthen empire as much as religion. In fact, the castle was over the border, on the Russian side, and from the first the Russians looked on askance, then indignant. Then they went to war—for decades. Practically for centuries, until they finally won the castle in 1714.

The siege took the Russians so long because there were miraculous things about this castle, even though Knut Posse did not put on a big bang when he ruled it. In the first place, Tott dedicated his castle to Olav, his patron saint. Olav had led the romantic, adventurous life of a pagan prince, conducting his first Viking expedition against the Swedes at the age of twelve, another, and then a third against Finland. But when Olav reached Finland the Finns conjured a storm and high seas for the night, and Olav escaped only because those good spirits hovering over him were stronger than any of the Finns' conjurings. After that Olav became a Christian and fell in battle, thus becoming Northern Europe's favorite saint.

More important than St. Olav's protection was probably the presence of that mermaid who rose at night out of the black waters of the sound and disturbed the silence of the night with her harp, like a siren enticing mortals to destruction, but giving warning, unlike the sirens of Odysseus, that a critical hour was at hand.

Probably the best help of all was that castellan who always walked the ramparts of his castle at midnight. He crept along in stocking feet to see if the guards were doing their duty—if he found a guard sleeping at his post he threw him over the rampart into the black water. And laughed his hollow, sardonic laughter. That laugh haunts the castle today.

I did not hear it. My guide had not heard it all summer long. But an American woman had offered a million marks for the ghost, so it must have been there. Now was the time, if any—late in the evening, nobody in the castle but my guide and me, our footsteps echoing hollowly along the stone floors.

No luck.

However, I did see the dungeons: you were tried in the courtroom, and as soon as your guilt was proved you were lowered on a rope through a hole in the floor to the dungeons below. Thirty-five feet. No way of escaping, or even of demanding a new trial.

We saw the mountain ash growing from a crevice in the wall below the knights' balcony. A castellan's daughter was buried alive in that wall, and the mountain ash grows on the spot, getting its strength from her blood and tears.

We inspected the prison chamber of the Prince of Oldenburg. Poor prince! For fifteen years Catherine the Great kept him in this little cell, the bed a little niche in the wall, scarcely big enough for a good-sized dog to sleep on. When the prince finally became crazed he was released, and the next day he was accidentally shot in the woods.

We saw the idyllic walled-in garden, with the stream flowing merrily through the middle, a graceful archway leading to the big courtyard—and right next to the archway a stone jutting out from the wall. The executioner's block, my guide told me. So we went to the crypt, rummaged through some barrels of dusty bones, and I picked out a very nice one. When anybody asks, I say it is Erik Axelsson Tott's.

Tott's castle began as a simple triangular fortification, with three round towers at the apexes. Later, more towers were added, others crumbled, bastions were built, barracks, a whole village where craftsmen turned out armor and clothes, bread and ale. Here Gunilla Bielke staunchly ruled for two years after her husband's death, not much perturbed that her castle had only three tables, twice as many benches, three candelsticks, fourteen copper kettles, three towels, and a few other necessaries. Now the castle is the scene of dances on St. Olav's day, of opera presentations in the big courtyard, and a mecca for tourists. A place of quiet beauty, with an especially lovely round chapel in one of the towers, and superb views framed in the round openings through which arrows and gunpowder and hot pitch flew at the approaching Russians. View of forest and water that spell the romance of Savonlinna. Hundreds of miles away the swamps and rivers form their chains of lakes. From Iisalmi and Kuopio, from the heights of Koli, from all the Northland the waters rush to meet at Savonlinna, to flow madly past St. Olav's castle, flow on, creating the magic Saimaa. Waters—mad, imprisoned, roaring down the Vuoksi, leaving a churning Imatra behind. Waters flowing on, eastward, to pour at last into the Ladoga.

But Lisa—I had almost forgotten her.

No, she was not at home. Of course I knew she had been married last winter? Regards? Lisa would certainly be delighted if I would call myself.

Perhaps. But I took the next train to Punkaharju.

Punkaharju is a thread of dusty road between the waters. Stone walls are covered with heavy moss, pine trees cover the slopes, and pine needles carpet the path up to Runeberg's hill. "A real wonder, dear Hebe," said Madame Runeberg, "very little mentioned, but incredibly beautiful." That was a century ago, at the time when Runeberg used to compare this spot with Hilda Holm, the loveliest lady he had ever seen or could ever imagine: "Put Hilda Holm on Punkaharju and you gather in one glance the most beautiful things that life and nature can offer."

Runeberg was a romantic. And I was sitting on Runeberg's hill in 1939. But alone. And I had no Hilda Holm (and even Lisa was married), no Karlheinz or his companions. Three years ago it had been different, but even three years ago I would not have stumbled on this spot if my Aunt Mimi had not cautioned me to visit Jyväskylä. Uncle Sem was already waving good-by when Aunt Mimi gave me her last words of repeated advice: "Be sure to visit Jyväskylä."

It is a charming city. Everyone who visits it will admit that. Aunt Mimi had studied there when she was young and spoke of the hard work and gay times. Women in Finland had but little higher education until Cygnaeus began to work for woman's equality with man and, some eighty years ago, founded the Jyväskylä Seminary. Here a woman was to be educated in such a fashion, Cygnaeus was careful to state, that she would retain her femininity and her feminine peculiarities. Around the school has grown a charming small city. It has that charm which comes from the simplicity and grace, the restfulness of the one-story wooden buildings, a harbor on the south, a background of hills and forests.

I waved good-by to Aunt Mimi and nodded my head. I would see Jyväskylä. But as the train pushed on the bright summer sky turned gray, and, without further hesitation, the rain began to pour down. The conductor walked past efficiently, proclaiming *Jyväskylä*. I took down my bag, looked out of the window to see Jyväskylä in the torrent of rain, charming and clean, the houses and trees glistening darkly wet, the cobblestone pavements gleaming maliciously. The city looked drenched and dreary. I put my bag up on the rack again, went to the end of the car, looked down once more, said "hello" to a chap who was looking at the town, too, and declared it was really raining. I offered him a cigarette, and we began talking. Five minutes later the train was still waiting. Did they expect someone to get off? And then it went on, past a place called Vaajakoski, with huge modern factories and smoke-stacks against the sky, into a long tunnel, through gloomy forests and narrow gorges cut in the granite, past lakes jammed with logs, over bridges, by a dozen small stations deep in the woods. Then the train stopped for good. We dashed through the rain, into the station restaurant, and went on talking and philosophizing.

Perhaps the rain and the gloom brought out my companion's pessimistic, Schopenhauerian nature. "Those forests and smoke-stacks," he brooded. "How closely they are related to each other! There is the average peasant, his home next to some evergreen and birch forest, and a lake or two, living in a small log house, suffering cold winters, eating poorly, always facing poverty. Doesn't he realize that three quarters of all Finland is forestland? The trees are ruthlessly cut down (but the government wisely keeps strict reforestation regulations) and the logs

are transformed into bobbins and matches and plywood, into wood-pulp and cellulose and paper.

"But," at this point the indignant young fellow,
intellectual, ardently patriotic, asked, "who owns
these rich factories? Foreigners," he immediately
added, not giving me a chance. And he went on to
prove how all the major industries were in foreign
hands. And what did the Finnish worker get out of
it? Nine cents an hour. And how much did butter
cost? Thirty cents a pound. Well then, and cigarettes? Six cents.

"That is not the only thing," the indignant intellectual went on. "We are Finns, but these businesses
have their leaders brought in from other lands. Why
don't we have a chance? Swedish is spoken in the
offices; accounts are kept in Swedish. Is it right?"

And so the fight is on to make Finnish the only
language of the country. My friend was an engineer.
He was young, and of course he had a future, but
he would never get an executive position in his firm
because he was Finnish. "Finland should be Finnish. . . ."

"Yes," I agreed. Of course, though these ardent
nationalists will have none of it, there are always two
sides to any question. I did not say anything about
it, however, for the map on the wall was more interesting. We were not far from Kuopio. Well, and

FINLAND

Jyväskylä? I could see that some other time. There was no point in going back: it was still raining. "I am going to Kuopio," I told my friend.

"Wish I could join you, but it's bobbins and spools for me."

I felt rather like a bobbin, too. The train shuttled and swayed, the rain beat against the windows, the light was poor for reading, the dampness made the car smell of varnish. It was dark and raining in Kuopio. I ran for a droshky, and we bumped along over old cobblestone streets to a hotel. When I awoke the sun was shining. I had my coffee and rolls in bed and wrote Aunt Mimi a card: "Jyväskylä was charming." Everyone who visits it will admit that, I mused, jumped out of bed and climbed up Puijo Hill.

Here I agreed with the guide-books for once: the view from the tower on Puijo Hill was wonderful. The whole countryside in every direction was covered with sparkling island-dotted lakes as far as the eye could see, on, past the horizon. The blue-green forests were magnificent. The city lay below us, set on the edge of a lake, gleaming in the sun. I say "us" because there was a group of Englishwomen on the tower. Such enthusiasm, momentary silence, and sudden rush of adjectives! A swift survey, and then, with that peculiar elasticity of the feminine mind (which I suppose Cygnaeus meant to preserve), they began talking just as earnestly and enthusiastically about their latest purchases in London's Caledonian Market.

In Kuopio there is nothing more to do once you have climbed Puijo Hill and praised the view to the natives, who all seem to expect that praise. Except have breakfast, walk around the streets for an hour or so, taking note of the vivaciousness of the peasant women in the market-place, the nondescript pleasantness of the streets, the curve of the lake shore as it skirts the city. The agreeableness of it all, not dependent on anything startling, just lakes and a hill, good food and good-natured people.

A quarter hour of bumping along the cobblestone streets in another droshky brought me to the harbor and the row of white lake steamers along the quay. I went over my plans quickly. Sailing at noon—on the *Haywater,* which promised finer scenery than the *Alderbrook*—I would be in Savonlinna the next morning. The trip would include good food and a few hours' sleep, but the steamship company particularly advertised the scenery, the winding of the boat through lakes, narrow channels, canal locks (operated by hand), by forested shores, past villas and farms and villages.

What the steamship line failed to advertise was the good company on board: a group of young Germans with their knapsacks and accordions, their short pants and gay songs; a maiden lady from Dublin, who was "doing" Finland and mothered me when she suspected I was catching cold; a girl from Savonlinna who took us all in hand, advised the young Germans, talked in French with the lady from Dublin, told me what I had to see on my trip. At one quay the lady from Dublin bought several baskets of raspberries. The girl from Savonlinna and I helped her eat them, and then she asked me to give some to the Germans. They retaliated by giving us a concert. It was a splendid concert, interspersed with candy munching, lots of cigarette smoke, running on deck to see something or other, and arguments for Hitler.

You cannot help but have a good time on these Finnish boats. On a trip that lasts an evening and a night you do not waste time with formalities. The boats are so small you see everyone in two minutes, and know them in five—everybody from the men who fire the boilers and the stewardesses to the bewildered cow on the forward deck sniffing at the bicycles and boxes and barrels to the chaps who have a portable phonograph on the lower deck (and American records three years old) or who play a concertina. Everybody sings and dances, or at least, looks on good-naturedly, except for the invariable pietist in black who frowns. You learn that so-and-so has just been to Turku and is going to Viipuri. You pester the captain with questions, crowding the bridge so the mate can hardly see if he is heading for a rock or a rowboat. The lady from Dublin offers you a "decent" cigarette (decent because they are English). After three months of Finnish tobacco they are so strong you cough. Have you caught a cold? It is actually cool, and you shiver involuntarily. She chides you for not having a heavier coat, takes you in tow, gives you aspirin and cognac and tells you to go straight to bed. But you go to another part of the deck to talk with the girl from Savonlinna whose name is Lisa.

I cannot tell you much about Lisa. Not even what she looked like: light hair, an ordinary nose, a few freckles, that is all. She had wanderlust, too. Not real desire for unimpeded adventure, but of the sort a nice girl can do—within bounds—like studying at the university, working in a factory, and social work. But all these things became boring to Lisa simply because they had to be done within bounds. Now she was trying marriage, but maybe that will become boring, too. She collected stamps, went to soccer games. We had little in common. But we were both determined that we would give the German boys a good time, and so it is that Karlheinz brought us together. It did not seem right to Lisa that the German boys should sleep every night in a tent and make their meals of bread and tea, though they were prepared to do these things and found enjoyment in them. Lisa invited the boys to a meal at her mother's, and arranged that in Savonlinna they should sleep at the YWCA. And the boys, intrigued by the prospects of a good meal, or by a girl who had something in common with them like collecting stamps, or the incongruous idea of sleeping in a YWCA, were delighted.

It was not at all unsuccessful. Saturday morning found us all getting off at Savonlinna. (The bewildered cow and a couple of the bicycles had disappeared during the night.) I assured the lady from Dublin I felt very much better, indeed, and waved her a cheery farewell. The pietist did not look a bit cheerful, however, even though it was a lovely day and he was in Savonlinna. The captain came to say good-by to us. Lisa went off to her mother's, and I went down the gangplank, with a dozen German lads in tow, and headed for the YWCA.

We saw the castle, whole-heartedly approving everything from the rowan tree growing from the blood and tears of the unfortunate maiden to the plumbing arrangements and the executioner's block in the garden. I admitted there were some fine castles in Germany, too. We walked through the *Kurpark*. I admitted Baden-Baden was very fine, and that my friends could feel as out of place here in shorts as I had done in Baden-Baden. We went to the market-place to buy dark bread and cheese for the next day's meals. We agreed it was a pleasant market-place, even though Gothic buildings did not surround it— only low wooden buildings on one side, the sound on the other, and a telephone booth in the middle. We walked out of the town to meet Lisa—she had asked us if we wanted to see a plywood factory, and we had all said yes. Lisa had worked in this factory herself for a few months, she explained, as she introduced us to the superintendent. He was Swedish, and though he knew how to talk Finnish, he preferred speaking German. (Perhaps my young friend on the train to Kuopio had been right, after all.)

It was an amazing factory. We were amazed by the fascinating progress of a birch log transformed into a beautiful plywood panel: logs pulled up from the lake, peeled into thin, sweet-smelling sheets, dried into crisp pieces like huge slabs of Melba toast, coated with hot glue and pressed against other slabs and dried again, sanded and polished and placed in neat stacks. We were amazed to learn that most of the panels went to England, there to be sawed and nailed into neat boxes, boxes that were sent empty to India and returned to Engand filled with tea. We were still more amazed to see all the work done by women: women dressed in bloomers and shorts and overalls. That is certainly feminine independence and equality. Did Cygnaeus intend it to go that far? We were all chivalrous lads, and felt uncomfortable and ashamed. We did not feel better about it until later, when we were playing darts in a corner of Lisa's garden and chivalrously wishing her victory.

I initiated the boys into the ritual of the *sauna*, amused at their desire to go into it whole-heartedly coupled with hesitation and doubt, then their enjoyment as the heat became greater and they beat themselves with the birch twigs, to the climax in that exhilarating plunge into the lake. And Lisa and I initiated Karlheinz into the mystery of Finnish cooking—with two maids and Lisa's mother looking on amused as we stirred the kettle over the hot stove and Karlheinz took notes. It was an excellent meal: porridge, fish pie, raspberries, coffee. The lads gave another concert, with no mention of Hitler, looked at Lisa's stamp collection, and trudged back to the YWCA.

The next day we took the train to Punkaharju and walked along the curling ridge. We became philosophical. At least, the lads put down their knapsacks with the flimsiest of pretenses—a new view or a shady grove—and we sprawled on the moss and pine needles and talked and smoked. We had a meal of bread and cheese even though it was early, for it is surprising how often you think of food when it is in a knapsack on your back. We walked a few kilometers more and had coffee at a little inn, for walking is no enjoyment if you cannot eat and drink. We

said *auf wiedersehen* there. The Germans hiked on
to Imatra, and I took a bus back to Savonlinna.

It was a fruitless return, because Lisa talked of
the Berlin Olympics, which I had carefully avoided,
and made me promise to send her some stamps. The
next morning I went to Imatra, too.

Imatra is a great place: "the mighty river Vuoksi,
and the Imatra terrific," the *Kalevala* describes it. A
dam captures the roaring Vuoksi, and the turbines
spin out electricity for all southern Finland, for
Helsinki, even for Turku. Imatra used to be a still
greater place when the torrents rushed wildly
through its rocky gorge, with a deafening roar proclaiming itself Europe's finest waterfall, when mortals (generally disappointed lovers) looking down
from the iron bridge above were so fascinated by the
whirling, enticing currents they used to sacrifice
themselves to the whirlpools in startling numbers.
But (sigh) that is no more. It is stern reality now, an
empty rocky gorge with a few stranded logs, and a
hundred and seventy-two-thousand horse-power har-
nessed to civilization. Only on Sundays can you see
the water roaring down, but even this service is not
arranged for the benefit of week-enders; it simply
means that on Sunday the power plant is idle. When
we saw Imatra on Monday, the gorge was drying out,
and the logs were caught in the rocks. And the only
anywhere near wild thing about was a gypsy girl:

she urged us to photograph her, and when we did, she insisted on being paid. It was all very picturesque, you see. Lured from fortune-telling or petty thievery, she stands here, photographed against an elemental setting of empty rocky gorge and forest and sky as a symbol of everything that is not Finnish.

Viipuri proved better. I went there that same afternoon to find a camping place for the *Wandervögel*. I went from consuls to police officials, from the fire department to the city treasurer's, unraveling knots, helping with suggestions, losing a little ground every time a new official learned I was not their collective guardian or even appointed guide, getting nearer my goal each time, until I was finally told they could camp on the Havi Bastions. Quite an interested audience turned out to see the Germans lift their tent—a crowd of curious boys, cherishing the idea of a tent in the middle of a city. A couple of old men, who did not know why a tent should be perched there and refused to believe anything would come of it, anyway. A policeman, in the course of duty. Myself, assuring the old chaps it would rise, all right; explaining to the policeman that permission had been granted; telling the curious boys about the strangers. I was impatient, eager to have the tent up so I could say to my friends, "Good—now what do you want to see in Viipuri?"

I was a good guide; I had spent half a day looking at the city.

"We ought to see the cemetery."

It was a request I had not expected. To choose the cemetery of all places to see in Viipuri—it was strange, but I only took a look at my map and said, "Let's go."

I found out what they were looking for. A monument: *den gefallenen deutschen Helden* . . . one of the many scattered throughout Finnish cities. Still, it was a queer way to see Finland, through its monuments to fallen Germans. My friends looked at it dutifully, without showing much interest. Perhaps it was just something a Nazi Baedeker insisted they must do, to bring home to these Hitler Youth the part that German soldiers had played in the Finnish war for independence, how heroically they had died in a strange land for the cause of humanity.

Bunk. Nothing of the sort. The Germans came with deeper motives. "Not Finnish, but purely German interests led our troops to Finland," declared Ludendorff.

Finland was to be freed from red Russian influence, yes, but in turn, it was whispered, the Germans expected Finland to become a monarchy with a German prince as king. The plans were all ready. The Finns were to vote: shall we have a king, or shall we have a president? The issue was decided when the

FINLAND

Germans lost the war: Finland became a republic. Now the German youth survey Finland, appraising lake and forest, envying Petsamo's nickel and Outokumpu's copper, and standing mute before memorials to the *gefallenen deutschen Helden*.

But Karlheinz and I did not speak of these things when he left the boys sleeping in the tent on the Havi Bastion and we walked through the twilight-dawn of Viipuri. We had more important things to talk about. Ourselves, our lives and enthusiasms, our ambitions and ideals. The books we had read, the girls we had kissed and the delights we had tasted. Frankly, as if we were old friends who had not seen each other in years. We learned all about each other and understood each other as we sat on the cliff overlooking the sea, listened to the music on the Torkel, and saw the dawn from the bastions.

I should have gone on to Valamo the next morning. I had a note from Lisa to one of the monks; he was to treat me well and show me everything. But I decided I might as well see Aunt Mimi and tell her about Jyväskylä, so I took the same train as my German friends. We parted company near Helsinki, with me standing on the station platform at Riihimäki, posing for the clicking cameras of my friends.

They must have made wonderful pictures: a young man with a plaid shirt and a Vandyke beard waving good-by.

94

III 〜

LAND OF HEROES

I PASSED through Jyväskylä again. It is as though we were fated not to meet each other, for I got no closer to the city than the station restaurant. At the same time I began to like Jyväskylä and could even say with some justice, "I love you, but what is that to you?" while I took malicious pleasure in wanting to stop but being obliged to pass through. This time I was hurrying to Mikkeli.

In Erich Lassota von Steblau's sixteenth-century listing of Finland's four castles and seven cities, in which he carefully names six and leaves the seventh an unsolved mystery, there is no mention of Mikkeli. Mikkeli is not this seventh, yet it is not an upstart, for not far away are the remains of a castle that Per Brahe half built in the Sixteen fifties, and a couple of months before the French stormed the Bastille the citizens of Mikkeli could hear the sounds of battle and were able to rejoice in victory over the Russians. Mikkeli is in the heart of Savo, one of Finland's historic provinces. It is also at the northwest edge of the Saimaa lake and can be reached by boat from Savonlinna in a roundabout but pleasant way. If you were to ask why anyone should visit Mikkeli when Baedeker mentions nothing more than "a view" from the top of the water tower, the answer is that it is the capital of Savo, a city that is provincial and pleasant and takes only the better features of modern civilization, like new buildings and water towers, and plants them serenely on the edge of the cobblestone streets, always near a park and trees and the breezes of the Saimaa.

You might also visit the little medieval chapel that is a museum and see the stone that marked the grave of Cesilia Eleanora Jägerhorn, 1752–1770. Young Cesilia was the toast of Mikkeli's aristocracy; she was loved miles around for her beauty and goodness, especially by the populace: I want to tell you the legend of Cesilia, for the masses build legends only around those they love. The first part of the tale ends when the eighteen-year-old Cesilia, while dancing gaily in her husband's arms on their wedding night, suddenly collapses and dies. The startling climax, however, came years later. One moonlit night, without any warning, the burgomaster of Mikkeli saddled his fine white horse, headed for the chapel and took the still beautiful body of Cesilia from its casket—and with her in his arms rode for hours through the city and the countryside. Then, just as suddenly, he returned to the chapel and laid Cesilia's form again to rest. The queer burgomaster was found dead in his bed the next morning.

When you have seen this chapel, climbed the

water tower for the "view," noted that there are five bookstores to one cinema, slept long, eaten well, and done nothing in particular to write your friends about, you might go to the lake front and pick a trim white steamer and a destination, knowing that you will find nothing more startling than peace.

The steamer I chose was a launch that consumed cord after cord of wood just to taxi farmers' wives and summer people between Mikkeli and the odd corners of the Saimaa lake. It was not an arduous schedule, for the steamer came around but once every day, and then so early in the morning that once I was settled in a far-off corner of the Saimaa I rarely took advantage of the opportunity to go back to Mikkeli. However, it was comforting to know that civilization was at your beck and call, though in such an unobtrusive fashion that you yawned and let civilization take care of itself. But this was Saturday morning, and half of Savo had come to Mikkeli to throng the market-place and to meet friends. When I made my way back to the pier the launch was full of baskets, bundles and peasant women. There was scarcely room enough for me to twist my head enough to see everything—the villas on wooded slopes, each with a *sauna* on the shore; the meadows; the narrow channels that did not look quite wide enough for our boat. Everyone took it complacently, though I expected the worst. The worst never came,

97

for it is said these Saimaa captains could pilot their ships through nothing deeper than the morning dew.

We stopped at practically every landing to deposit a basket or a box—or at least a newspaper. Then we crossed a wider stretch of lake sprinkled with rocks, with a little red villa high on a hill in the background. We stopped there, too, to let me off. I had come to my friends' villa after frantic letters asking about my arrival had pursued me all over Finland— they were not afraid I had been lost so much as they were anxious to show the hospitality that everyone in Finland shows. Even an afternoon call means staying long enough for a cup of coffee, which means three cups—make two or three calls, multiply the coffee, the offers of dinner, the suggestion you stay at least overnight or better yet a week, the reproaches of "Do you mean to say you have come all the way to Finland and are only staying two weeks with us?" and you have the measure of Finnish hospitality. I thought a week was all I could spare for the Saimaa villa, but immediately I had to agree to at least two weeks. It would be a restful fortnight of swimming and *sauna* and conversation.

For the first day it was all of that. My hostess wrote novels; my host rested from his task of directing a big school by carrying rocks and writing speeches. Their two sons spent the day between swimming and writing—Tuuri, seventeen, turning out lurid stories of crime and adventure for provincial newspapers; Aije, twelve, editing a newspaper with an exciting story that continued in installments of one intense paragraph from issue to issue. Tonia, the secretary, seemed to divide her time between arranging flowers and typing letters. And I sat in a beach chair in the sun and said I was writing a book about Finland.

It was a "busy" life. At nine we would have coffee and talk and drink more coffee for an hour and a half. Then everyone went off to work industriously —for the half hour before breakfast. An hour more of work brought afternoon coffee, and guests, and so two more hours disappeared in the company of dowagers or art critics; in visits to the post-mistresses' vacation home, a camp for underprivileged children, or a home for invalid war veterans; in talk with professors and flyers and the man in the country store. Usually there was not much time left for work before dinner, but we made the most of it. After evening coffee the sunset over the lake seemed more important than work: it lingered on for hours, until we finally had to go to bed. Somehow, though, the speeches managed to be written. Tuuri's stories brought in checks, and Aije's newspaper turned out on time. My hostess worked half the night in her study down by the lake, and I went to bed every night saying I really ought to write my book. I did get as far as jotting down a note about the big rock that loomed out of the water near the middle of the lake.

That was no ordinary rock. Years ago in the wilderness of Savo there had been a boy and a girl who had loved each other with all the passion of youth. But the lad was poor, the girl rich, her parents unyielding. The lovers eloped one night, in a little skiff. Far from angry parents, they landed on this little rock and slept a blissful sleep. But in the morning—the skiff was gone and the lovers were left to perish on the rock. It is an old legend, and many rocks from one end of the Saimaa to the other are claimed as "the spot." This was the authentic one, however, for I dreamed I floated there on a raft that was a book about Finland, and in the morning there was no raft. After that I spent fifteen minutes less at morning coffee and moved my beach chair into the shade.

This could have gone on and on, but my hostess was anxious to show me as much of Savo as possible. We went across the lake in hot sun and cold rain, into places where there was no morning dew to cover the rocks; we motored over highways for hours, to attend some meeting; we plunged through forests to backwoods settlements, until it did not matter whether the beach chair was in the sun or in the shade. Young Aije characterized the spirit of our wanderings at the beginning, when he insisted on going with us to a patriotic meeting, declaring, "I want to get acquainted with the fatherland——"

This fatherland, as an independent nation, is twenty-two years old, vital and young. But there were centuries of preparation, and dreaming that seemed almost hopeless of fulfillment, a long prelude of toil and sorrow and oppression before the goal was attained.

One important phase of this struggle was the penetration of the vast wilderness of Finnish forest by pioneers. In Savo, for example, pioneering meant not only leaving a home and friends for the task of wresting a new strip of field from the forest and building a new home, but the systematic colonization of a bulwark against the line the Russians claimed for their own. Savo began as a wilderness so vast that "fugitive prisoners could hide themselves there for five, six, nine years, until time wiped out the memory of the guilt or old age brought pardon." So successful was this penetration of the wilderness that a century later, in 1617, Gustav Adolph could truthfully say that since Finland and Russia were separated by the Ladoga, "I hope it will be no easy task for the Russians to jump over this puddle."

This colonization was so successful that a few years later, when Gustav Adolph went off to uphold Swedish glory and the Protestant cause in the Thirty Years' War, his army was largely made up of Finns. The sturdy men of Savo won Gustav's battles and then were so amazed at the easy-going life of the Rhineland and the products of the vineyards that they lost all desire to return to their native Savo.

The Savoans were so adept at clearing the wilderness that when Gustav Adolph decided to plant a colony in the Delaware River valley—with trade as the incentive, colonization as a possibility, and missionary work as a vague suggestion—the Finns took an integral part in this earlier settlement of America. They were great hunters, these Finns, stanch individualists, skilled in magic; "forest-destroying Finns" who cleared land by simply burning away the forests. As soon as the colony began to flourish, the envious Dutch grabbed it. Having a grudge against the Dutch, the English annexed the territory, and William Penn sailed up the peaceful Delaware and was pleased with the Finns whom he found on his land. He declared them a "plain, strong, industrious people—proper and strong of body, so that they have fine children and almost every house full . . . I see few young men more sober and industrious." The Finnish towns of Upland and New Finland duly became Chester and Marcus Hook, and the Finns almost disappeared from American history as such, until the new waves of immigration in the late nineteenth century.

That later immigration came because the dream of Finnish independence was being ruthlessly crushed by the Russians, although this dream that had been smoldering for hundreds of years was never completely stamped out. In the sixteenth century Gustav Vasa realized that Sweden's rule over Finland was not an inevitability of nature, that on the contrary, Sweden had to earn Finland's acceptance of any ties and bonds between the two by her good actions. Per Brahe came to carry out these good actions, and as a result, Finland became an integral part of the Swedish state, a Grand Duchy ruled by the same laws that governed Sweden, taxed the same, and bravely fought Sweden's wars, with no hesitation, no feelings of grievance or exploitation, no resentment at dying on the battlefields of Pultava or Leipzig. It was not until later—when Sweden seemed to be weakening; when, grasping at straws, she challenged the Russians to a series of wars which resulted in just as regular a series of defeats for the Swedes; when the battlefield was always Finnish soil and meant the periodic destruction of everything that had been patiently built up from the Finnish wilderness—that the Finns began to dream of independence for themselves.

FINLAND

The Empress Elizabeth of Russia first hinted the possibility of independence to the Finns in a manifesto in 1742: though Russia wanted nothing more than to be on peaceful and neighborly terms with Sweden, these Swedes unfortunately were always provoking her to war, to Finland's detriment. Of course Russia was in the right since she always won and since God always favored the cause of the just. Therefore, if the Finns wanted to declare Finland free, independent and self-governing, she, Elizabeth, would help them to achieve this freedom. The proposition led to nothing, since there seemed to be some doubt as to Elizabeth's real motives.

Sweden continued getting weaker reign by reign. A king might start his career there as a great warrior and find that at the end of his reign he was acknowledged a "skillful hunter" at the most. But when Gustav III left Paris in 1771 to receive his crown at the age of twenty-five, he determined to do better. He was a handsome fellow, the idol of Europe's courts, with all the glitter and polish of a French education, including arrogance, the ability to spend money, and a fondness for theatricals. He was a good fellow, interesting at stag parties. The French naturally urged this likable prince to be a real king, but his uncle in Potsdam, Frederick the Great, warned him to behave so discreetly, at least, that Russia would not become his enemy. When Gustav reached Stockholm his friends again urged him to be a real king and offered to stage a revolution that would take the power out of the hands of parliament and put it in his lap. Gustav knew that Catherine the Great of Russia was no real menace at this time, for she was occupied with threatening the Turks and partitioning Poland. George Magnus Sprengtporten went home to Finland, ostensibly to help the Finns solve their salt shortage. He staged a revolution instead. Parliament was immediately dissolved, and Gustav became a real king. Frederick shook his head, and Catherine was vexed.

The grateful Gustav sent Sprengtporten back to Finland as the commander of the Savo forces. His task was to build up Finland—which meant he was to build up the army. He did, starting a military school at his Brahe castle headquarters near Mikkeli, and working so enthusiastically that the fame of his school soon spread through Europe. Gustav became jealous and sent his friend to look at the armies of Moscow, Berlin and Paris. In Paris Sprengtporten resigned from the king's service—he had just become acquainted with Benjamin Franklin and was so moved by the reports of the struggles of the American colonies for independence that he wanted to go to America to fight. Since he couldn't do this, he returned to Finland to dream of a similar independence for his country.

FINLAND

Gustav grew more powerful at home and seriously began to look outward for "a war worthy of his reign," to raise Sweden to that position in international prestige it had enjoyed a century earlier. He asked Catherine if it would be all right to war on Denmark, but Catherine frowned on this, for Denmark was her ally. And so, without more ado than to note that Catherine was more tied up with the Turks than ever, Gustav decided to fight Russia. Some Swedish soldiers, masquerading as Russians, crossed the border near Mikkeli, firing a few stray shots into the Swedish ranks. This "incident" was proof enough that the evil Russians were bent on a horrible offensive war. Shortly after that the enemy fleets met in front of Suursaari (Hogland: the Big Island) in a five-hour combat: both sides reported a naval victory, and the war was on.

Finnish opposition crystallized early. Sprengtporten remembered his conversations with Franklin and entertained vague notions of a republic patterned after the United States. Two years before Gustav's war started, Sprengtporten went to Russia to suggest this move for independence to Catherine. She received him well, showered favors on him, and added him to her armies as a major-general. In the meantime his friend Johan Jägerhorn (was he the husband of the unfortunate Cesilia Eleanora?) carried on the work in Finland, starting the "Valhalla

Order" of liberal officers who dreamed of an independent Finland. As soon as the war broke out these officers signed the Liikala Note, bringing assurances to Catherine that this war was distasteful to the Finns, who loved peace and wanted Catherine to bring it about. A few days later these officers sent the Anjala Declaration to Gustav, strongly urging him to end the war.

Gustav was left in a peculiar position that made him almost a prisoner in the hands of the Finnish army. His salvation came when he received word that Denmark was mobilizing for a war against Sweden.

"*Je suis sauvé!*" Gustav exclaimed. He was free to dash off to protect Sweden, without making his departure look like flight.

The Finnish campaign was left in the hands of Gustav's brother. He was ready enough to listen to the Anjala proposals, and perhaps he began to think of himself as king of Finland. All might have gone well, except that Russia suddenly urged an immediate session of the Finnish parliament to proclaim Finland's independence—as a protectorate of Russia.

The eyes of the Finns were suddenly opened. The officers of the Anjala league were discredited as traitors, and the Finns began to fight in earnest. It was a brilliant beginning. A couple of months before the French stormed the Bastille, some seven hundred Finnish soldiers halted an army of eight thousand Russians at Porrassalmi, near Mikkeli. This startling success, however, was followed up by only a few minor skirmishes, and a *status quo ante* peace was soon declared. An "eternal" peace.

Finland gave up her thoughts of independence.

Today the Civil Guard and the Lotta Svärd, the women's auxiliary to the guard, see to it that nobody shall forget Finland's independence. As a pacifist (remembering that in America the National Guard is called out by vested interests every now and then to put down a strike by throwing tear-gas bombs and cracking a few skulls) such organizations had seemed distasteful to me. Of what use could such an organization be, an "elite guard" that minds everybody's business with a tone of righteousness? But Finland's independence was not won without a struggle, and these organizations felt it might not be maintained without further struggle. (They were right.) This summer, with everybody digging ditches on the Carelian frontier, these organizations turned to the public with greater effectiveness. They were having a festival at Mäntyharju, and Aije and I were going there to "get acquainted with the fatherland."

It was a warm rainy evening, and we could easily have forgotten the fatherland and its problems in the stuffy atmosphere of the small auditorium if we had not been sitting on hard, backless benches which

forced a certain show of backbone and attention.
There was music by a band and a string trio, a poem
recited by a blushing student, a play that produced
laughs intentional and otherwise, a good speech, then
a speech by a young fellow who said he was writing
a book about Finland. By that time everybody was
impatient for the evening's dancing to begin, but
there were prizes to be given, including a doll
dressed as a Lotta Svärd that came to the young
author's share. The doll's name was Elina, and I
could think of nothing but another Elina whose husband had burned her to death. It was a successful
evening, Aije decided.

Our next encounter with the fatherland was different. A farmhouse deep in the Savo wilderness was
our goal, reached after a long boat ride, a longer walk
through dense forest, and a swim in a lake so inviting
we could not resist wasting time. The farmhouse was
an ordinary one, but fresh paint inside and out was
a sign of self-respect and even prosperity; it was old
enough to make the one automobile next to the barn
look out of place—it had brought the two fat ladies
who were Lotta Svärd leaders in the city. Most of
these hard-working peasants had come miles on foot,
just as we had, perhaps to see their friends, but
chiefly because they loved their land. The boys
looked at the automobile as if it were much more
useless than a plow. The men ignored it completely

FINLAND

and clustered in a group to talk about crops. The women were sitting on the porch, and most of the old people with wrinkled hands and faces had already taken their places on the hard benches set up in the long kitchen. You might conceive hard-working American farmers assembling for a prayer meeting or corn husking, but who could imagine American farmers getting together like these Finnish peasants, tired after a week of toil, to listen to speeches about such seemingly remote problems as their nation's defense?

One of the fat Lotta Svärd ladies made a speech: a cold, unemotional speech, haltingly read in a voice that stubbornly trailed high when she wanted to end sentences. The young author who said he was writing a book about Finland became enthusiastic, quite Finnish, and urged more and better ditches on the Carelian frontier. Then a pale, young, Dimmesdale-like minister made a speech: he began in an unimpassioned tone, but suddenly he grew dramatic, forgetting such immaterial possibilities as the help of God to state that a small nation can guard itself only with its own strength, directed with a single purpose to a single goal. I had visions of this pale young man carrying huge boulders to the wall that was the Russian frontier. "We are not Czechoslovakia," he declared, "and it is better to die on the gallows than to live a slave!"

This outburst of the pale young minister was certainly militant. "It is better to die on the gallows than to live a slave" has for generations been on the lips of the Finnish people, whose very struggle for existence has been the fight against oppression and enslavement. They were not Swedes and they did not want to become Russians, so they tried hard to be Finns. As long as they were under Sweden they could at least dream of independence, but when Russia annexed Finland the case began to look hopeless. The Swedish kings were to blame.

When Gustav III could not find the war that was to be worthy of his reign, he turned to other matters, including the counterfeiting of Russian money, but chiefly to a display of sympathy for the French royalty, which was being rapidly guillotined. This sympathy earned Gustav nothing more than a pistol shot in the back at a masked ball, and his fourteen-year-old son, Gustav IV, took the throne. A benevolent eye was immediately turned to Finland: there was an attempt to better conditions by forbidding all use of silk and coffee and by founding schools in Lapland. As soon as Gustav IV was old enough to rule without a regent, he began to feel the divine right of kings, and as a king he tried to become the arbiter of Europe's affairs. He succeeded in becoming Europe's laughing-stock. He did not like England, because the British had been nasty to Swedish shipping. He could not get along with Russia or Tsar Alexander, even though Alexander was his brother-in-law. He hated France and despised the "Corsican traitor" with increasing bitterness—if no one else was ready to fight Napoleon, Gustav was willing to do it alone, heroically. He appealed to Alexander, and Alexander gave him an army.

Napoleon had just been victorious at Jena: Prussia was crushed. The French chased Gustav to Stralsund, then to Rügen, and he was on the brink of defeat when Alexander met Napoleon at Tilsit to sign a non-aggression pact. With the characteristic passion for detail that dictators possess, Napoleon remembered Sweden and decided to ruin Gustav. It was easy: Napoleon turned over the task of chastising Gustav to Alexander, who was to take Finland for his pains. After all, Finland was Russia's "geographical enemy"; furthermore, Finland's boundary was too close to St. Petersburg—surely Alexander realized the noise of cannon thundering on the border disturbed the lovely ladies in their St. Petersburg palaces?

Alexander did not know quite how to go about his task. Besides, the lovely ladies in their St. Petersburg palaces said, "Fie, it is not sportsmanlike." Napoleon grew insistent, however, and Alexander had to make a move. He urged Gustav to join his armed neutrality league against England and close the Baltic to British ships. That was in October, 1807, and when Gustav showed no desire to accept the suggestion, Alexander invaded Finland the following February. A winter campaign would not be too difficult for the Russian soldiers.

Gustav made no defense preparations. On the contrary, he had decided to leave Finland to its fate while he made plans to conquer Norway with England's help. However, he did send a commander, Count Klingspor, to take charge of the Finnish army. Klingspor was old and timid, and Gustav's orders had been to save as much of the army as possible by a retreat to northern Finland, leaving a door open for flight into Sweden. The Finns shook their heads —they were not as timid as Klingspor. As soon as the Cossacks nipped at the feet of the retreating army, the Finns turned back and fought—victoriously— with Klingspor looking on in amazement. Perhaps it could be done, perhaps Finland could be saved. The Finns needed more men; Gustav used them to fight Norway. The Finns needed supplies; Gustav sent word to the officers they need not powder their wigs during the winter campaign. It could have been done. The Finns fought valiantly, but Gustav sent no help. In 1809 Finland was lost, and Gustav, His Majesty, King of Sweden, "felt released of the responsibilities" of looking after the Finns. What he turned over to the Russians was, as a Russian put it,

FINLAND

"a state and no government." For a century the Russians kept it that way—a state without a government.

It was not a state without patriots, however. Confusion gave way to oppression, and the Finns who had not been Swedes were more certain than ever that they did not want to become Russians. They had to be Finns.

"They *were* Finns," concluded Runeberg, Snellman and Lönnrot, those three noble men whom the University at Turku produced before it burned down, literally as well as spiritually, and moved to Helsinki to go on its way as the Royal Alexander University.

Johan Ludvig Runeberg was not a great poet. There have been better poets in Finland, but none so revered as Runeberg. His *Songs of Ensign Stål* became a popular epic as soon as it was published, for here was the war of 1808 in heroic proportions, written in the lives of the men—and women—who tried to save Finland. Each succeeding generation of Finns has been spellbound by these songs. My father learned them when he was a schoolboy, and he can still repeat them word for word. At the age of four Runeberg saw the Finnish leader von Döbeln, who urged the fleeing Klingspor to turn back and fight, threatening heaven with a clenched fist and cursing the skies that gave him no rain to save his men; he

sat on the knees of the Russian Kulnev, who pursued
Klingspor with a Cossack horde. Never could he forget these childhood memories of von Döbeln with
the black band across his forehead or Kulnev with
his long black beard: these memories were fired by
the strong flame of patriotism which burned in his
heart and resulted in a tired old man, Ensign Stål,
sitting by the fire, singing of the glorious von Döbeln
and the heroes who thronged about him to save Finland. Some of them were aristocrats; some, stable
boys and farmhands. One of them was Lotta Svärd,
who followed her husband into war. All of them
were human, but more than that, they were brave,
and they fought heroically—because they believed in
Finland. They sacrificed everything in the fervent
hope that Finland might be saved:

"I saw a people who were able to do everything
except betray their honor. I saw an army, suffering
from cold and hunger, but victorious."

Runeberg appealed to the people as a poet, Snellman as a realist. When the *Songs of Ensign Stål* appeared, Snellman was already at the forefront of
Finnish life, at the critical moment when this life
seemed to be completely doomed to the peace of
death. With a dictatorial hand the Russians were
ready to crush anything that signified unrest. They
ruled the country through the Swedish leader class,
under inherited, sterile Swedish laws and culture.

FINLAND

(What was still worse—the attempt to impose Russian laws and culture—did not come until later. When it came, it was explosive.) There had been a time when Finland was Finnish: that was in the early days when the heritage of Finnish language and culture was kept alive by the people. In Carelia, for example, there was nothing Swedish: a seventeenth-century Viipuri governor had resigned his post because he could not speak Finnish. Later that inability became a minor consideration, and by the nineteenth century the Swedish snobbism of Turku was insidiously killing the Finnish spirit. Swedish was the language of the overbearing officials: Swedish was the language of the smug bourgeosie, whose only pride was their individual well-being and their ability to speak the polite Swedish. The preservation of Swedish custom and tradition became the only care of the aristocracy. But the majority of people—the peasants and farmers—were Finnish and spoke Finnish. There were few schools where they could learn their language, and often years passed by without any new Finnish books appearing besides an almanac and perhaps a book of sermons. The Russians approved the situation, the Swedish minority approved it, and the Finns did nothing about it until Snellman came upon the scene.

Johan Wilhelm Snellman—school principal, later a professor, then a senator—began the battle against

this doom. He was an idealist, a thinker and a statesman, but he was also a realist and a fighter. Snellman, who was born of Swedish-speaking parents and
always wrote in Swedish, was, paradoxically, more
than any person a Finn at heart. With patriotic ardor
he battled to awaken the Finnish soul, to bring the
Finnish language to a position of cultural, political
and social prestige.

The battle became a crusade. Snellman began a
newspaper, the *Saima,* and its voice "echoed through
Finland to awaken the Finnish people from its sleep
like the clarion call on judgment day." He knew
there could be no nation when no national feeling
existed; he knew that the living feeling of nationalism could not be kindled before the language of that
people became the accepted cultural language. He
forced the Finnish language into schools and law
books; he preached a national culture. Despair gave
way to hope. The students flocked to his banners;
the nation was aroused. Snellman became a god:
"Gentlemen! The magic Sampo which the *Kalevala*
heroes sought in vain—the Sampo which was to bring
them happiness, the magic secret which all men have
searched for from time immemorial—this Sampo has
now been found. It is not copper or lead; it is not
gold or silver. It is—our love for our people!"

This love was made easier by the appearance of
the *Kalevala,* the Finnish epic which appeared in

print in 1835, collected from the *runos* of scores of singers in backwoods, primitive Carelia and skillfully welded together by Elias Lönnrot, Finland's Homer. Its appearance signaled the rebirth of Finnish poetry, but more than that, revealed to the Finns the culture which was their heritage.

Lönnrot was born in a hut, one of a poor tailor's many children. As a boy he had to beg, eat bread flavored with bark and moss. He suffered jibes and taunts, and once some Russian soldiers threw him in a well. Then an older brother helped him, and Lönnrot went to school and then to the university. He wanted to become a doctor, but he did not want a fashionable practice. He sought and received the position of town doctor in isolated Kajaani, on the borders of Carelia, where he had an income and plenty of time to go through the countryside—hundreds of miles every year, on foot, by boat, on skis or in a reindeer-sled—to collect the old songs and ballads, the *runos* and proverbs which this isolated people, far from schools and prim Lutheranism, still had on its lips.

The fifty *runos* of the *Kalevala*, the Land of Heroes, tell the story of four Finnish heroes. The epic begins with the minstrel Wäinämöinen's birth "by a nameless promontory, near a barren, treeless country." Under his care the country grew into a land with trees, and birds singing in the branches; it grew into a land with herbs and flowers, berries and grain. Wäinämöinen passed his life in song, and his reputation spread far and wide, until it aroused the jealousy of Joukahainen, a young lad who was proud of his own singing and resentful that someone else should be counted better than he. The two minstrels met; Joukahainen challenged Wäinämöinen in song and lost—he saved himself from Wäinämöinen's spell only by promising him his sister Aino as a bride.

Aino would have nothing to do with Wäinä-möinen: she committed suicide. That made the hero want a bride more than ever: he journeyed to Pohjola, the Northland, for

> Lives in Pohjola a maiden,
> In that village cold a virgin.
> Who will not accept a suitor,
> Mocks the very best among them.
> Half of all the land of Pohja
> Praises her surpassing beauty:
> From her temples shines the moonlight,
> From her breasts the sun is shining.

Louhi, Pohjola's mistress, was willing to give Wäinä-möinen her daughter—if he could forge her a Sampo, "on one side a corn-mill, on another side a salt-mill, and upon the third a coin-mill." Wäinämöinen shook his head, but he offered to send his brother Ilmarinen, a smith without an equal, the most accomplished of the craftsmen. Ilmarinen forged to Sampo, but the maid of Pohjola was reluctant to marry. Ilmarinen returned home—alone.

The scene changes. The bold, handsome young Lemminkäinen takes the stage. He was not wholly faultless, "but was careless in his morals, passing all his time with women." He married a beautiful island girl after a whirlwind courtship and abduction. He lost her and went to woo Pohjola's maiden, enchanting everyone as he went, except one wicked cowherd. He plied his suit, but with no more success than Wäinämöinen, who was the best of minstrels, or Ilmarinen, who had forged the Sampo for the Northland. He could have the proud maiden if he captured the evil one's elk. He could have her if he bridled the evil one's fire-breathing steed. He could have her if he shot the swan on the black river of Tuonela, the land of the dead. During this third task the wicked cowherd whom Lemminkäinen had not enchanted killed him and threw his body into the river. His mother restored him to life, and he went sadly homeward—without the maid of Pohjola.

Wäinämöinen sails for the Northland once again to woo the maid, and Ilmarinen rushes there on horseback. Wäinämöinen fails completely, but before Ilmarinen receives the maiden's hand he must likewise perform three tasks: plow a field of serpents, capture the bear of Tuonela, catch the pike in Tuo-

nela's river. He succeeds. The mistress of Pohjola
sighs, and wedding preparations begin: a mammoth
ox is slaughtered, a huge pavilion is built, ale is
brewed, and heroes from all the land are invited.

The most unfortunate hero, however, was Kullervo, born of a noble but enslaved mother. Morose,
sullen, of great strength and greater rebelliousness,
he was sold to Ilmarinen for two worn-out kettles
and a half-dozen useless rakes and scythes. Ilmarin-
en's proud wife made the slave her herdsman, baked
stones in his bread, and sent him off to herd the
cattle. Enraged, Kullervo killed the cattle, sent
wolves and bears into the stable to tear Ilmarinen's
wife to pieces. He found his parents whom he had
thought lost; he tried hard to help them but brought
only disaster, his sister's ruin, his home's destruction,
and finally, in remorse, his own suicide.

Ilmarinen mourned for his dead wife. He found
no consolation in a golden image of her, but when
he went to Pohjola to woo his first wife's younger
sister, he was insulted and sent home with contempt
and sneering. They were contented in the Northland, for they had the Sampo, Ilmarinen complained
to his brother, and with it, "there was plowing, there
was sowing, there was every kind of increase—and
their welfare is eternal."

The three Kalevala heroes—Wäinämöinen, Ilmarinen and Lemminkäinen—sailed once more to Poh-

jola, this time to seize the Sampo. They succeeded, for the people were so enchanted by Wäinämöinen's harp and his magic songs they could do nothing. The men of Pohjola recovered from the spell that had been cast over them and pursued the men of Kalevala: there was a battle at sea, and the Sampo fell into fragments on the waves. Wäinämöinen collected the fragments, sowed them carefully in the hills and valleys that the land might flourish. Pohjola sent disease and pestilence; Wäinämöinen healed his people. Pohjola sent a bear to destroy their herds; Wäinämöinen killed the bear. Pohjola captured the sun and the moon, and locked them in a mountain; they were released, and there was peace in Kalevala. Peace, until suddenly the Virgin Marjatta swallowed a cranberry—and gave birth to a child. An old man baptized this child "the king of all Carelia, and the lord of all the mighty." Wäinämöinen was grieved and angry. He sang one song more, and sailed away forever:

> The kantele he left behind him,
> Left his charming harp in Suomi,
> For his people's lasting pleasure,
> Mighty songs for Suomi's children.

The *Kalevala* itself is a mighty song of heroes, but it is significant that the heroes' exploits are not of the sword, but deeds accomplished by song, by the knowledge of the power of words. The Sampo was forged with song, captured with another song, its fragments sown with still a third. Lemminkäinen won the maidens' hearts with songs; Kullervo brought disaster with his mad incantations. Patriarchal Wäinämöinen left the Finns a heritage of songs so mighty that "lakes swelled up, the earth was shaken; and the coppery mountains trembled, and the mighty rocks resounded." Songs so sweet that "all the leaves called gaily to him, and the heath was all rejoicing; the flowers breathed their fragrance round him, and the young shoots bowed before him."

Almost a divine comedy, in a setting that is at once a dreamland and an intensely real setting of meadow and farmhouse, of lake and a *sauna* on the forest's edge, the heroes of the *Kalevala* were not divine. It was not until centuries later that Michael Agricola mistakenly called them pagan gods. Actually the *Kalevala* is the story of life in southwestern Finland in the ninth and tenth centuries, with its raids into Lapland and its pillaging of Pohjola (the Swedish Gotland), its tale of the life and death of men and women, of wars and the peaceful *sauna,* the herding of cattle and the holding of feasts. It tells of the bareness of the Northland, the bleak and the cold, the long winter night when the sun and the moon are away in captivity, and the bright summer that knows no night. It tells of the coming of Christianity, with Marjatta swallowing a cranberry to give birth to the Christ child, sending pagan heroes into mourning exile.

The publication of the *Kalevala* in 1835 gave the Finns their heritage which most of them had forgotten: the heritage of a free political nation and a flourishing culture which Christianity and a new society had pushed into oblivion. It ushered in a renaissance more powerful than that awakening which had begun two centuries earlier with the founding of Turku's university: "You were awakened from your winter sleep by song, my Finland; the great poets echoed in your ears, my people, and the old songs of the ancestors tore the sleep from your eyes." It brought hopes, as yet slim, of a day when Finland would be independent again.

It is useless to speculate on what might have happened to the course of history if—enough that the Swedes did come to Finland on their worldly-motivated crusade. The Finns were made to forget they had possessed a language, that they had been free men and had developed a free culture, for Finland was made into something different, into a satellite of Sweden. The Swedes took advantage of Finland's potentialities, but then they drained the state they had built of life and wealth and hope until Sweden herself became a weakling among nations and Finland became a pawn in the hands of Russia.

Russia could not be blamed for wanting peace and quiet in her new province: she ruled the Duchy according to its old laws, she fretted that these laws were not Russian, she began to tear them down—one by one.

The Swedes in Finland could not be blamed for clinging tenaciously to the Swedish tradition—it was better than being Russian; it was surely better than trying to appear Finnish, for that would have meant appearing as the underdog lashed by Russian officialdom and despised by Swedish snobbism.

And the Finns could hardly be blamed for being Finns. They had a language once—they wanted it again. They had a culture once—they did not despise it. They had been free—they would be free once more.

NORTHERN NIGHT

ELISENVAARA, according to the guide-books, is a
"railway junction (station restaurant)." It is nothing but a sprawling, wooden building stretched out
along the half-dozen pair of railroad tracks that creep
out of the forest and disappear into it again. A water
tank and huge stacks of sawed, neatly piled logs are
waiting for the trains that steam up with bravado
and grind to a halt. Somewhere behind that forest
there may be a town with lakes, an old church, a
store or two, and a quiet air, but the junction gives
no sign of it. It is simply a breathing spell on a long,
interminable trip through league after league of
forest that has no beginning and no end.

The passengers pour into the station restaurant
for a meal. There is plenty of time, time to eat and
enjoy a leisurely cigarette, time to think of the hours
that must pass before the next long stop. I was going
north to Petsamo and the Arctic Ocean, and there
would be long monotonous hours in the train, many
junctions and stops where I would almost run into
the restaurant, gulp down some food, and discover
that I had plenty of time for a cigarette. Time there
is unimportant: you cannot imagine an hour or a
minute when you will finally be out of the reach of

tree after tree growing solidly beside the tracks. You measure time and distance by the fact that the Helsinki papers are a day late, that at the next long stop they are later still. And the news—Russia wanting to guarantee Finland's independence; Hitler ready to defend the Germans in Poland; Italy threatening to win the international soccer match—however ominous they look on the paper, lose their force when you are removed from the theater of ominous acts and dire foreboding, when you are as enchanted, rolling through the endless forest.

At the junction where the Helsinki papers are a day and a half late (I do not remember its name; it was a junction, surrounded by desolate stretches of forest, at a place where you would least expect a junction) crowds of people got on the train. I had to draw my feet away from under the other seat, where they had been comfortably stretched; I had to help ladies with their luggage; I had to get well into my corner, then out of it again to exchange a pleasant word of greeting. I was going to Vaala.

"Splendid—so are we," the two ladies opposite me explained, then wandered off into their own conversation.

The three old maids (they were from Philadelphia) across the aisle were going straight to Petsamo. They complained about the weather; really, there should be more air.

A young fellow from Chicago was going to Vaala —did I have reservations at the hotel?

A girl sitting alone in the far corner did not say anything: she stared out of the window.

I almost got into my corner again, but the old gentleman next to me began to talk. He was not going to Vaala, he was not on his way to Petsamo, he was going home to Oulu. In this crowd of people wandering aimlessly through the forests, to Vaala, to Petsamo, to whom time and distance meant only that they were in motion, that papers from Helsinki were a day and a half late, it seemed strange that someone should have home for a goal, and know when he would get there, at six o'clock or at seven, to find his wife waiting, and supper on the table.

I looked more closely at the old gentleman, at his round pink face, his thin gray hair, the wart rooted on the edge of his lower lip, his pudgy hands, the heavy gold ring. He looked hot and tired in his dark suit, very stiff collar, high black shoes. I was glad his wife would be waiting with supper on the table. He taught history at a high school in Oulu. You might assume he was on his way home from an educational conference. But no!

"I have been at the Carelian frontier," he replied. "Two weeks—for two weeks I have been digging trenches on the border. It is hard work for a man of sixty-five," he sighed. Here was a tired old man, a schoolmaster, who had sacrificed his vacation doing the hardest kind of physical work. He did not look upon himself as a hero: he had merely done his part that the Finns might remain Finns. There was a proud gleam in his eye: he was not afraid, he did not suspect defeat.

"I would have stayed longer," he went on, "but I am not used to work like that. The doctors said I had done enough. They gave me a free ticket home."

I felt more buoyant. What if I had been a night and a day in the same train, wandering through forest that looked the same for hundreds of miles? I explained to the two Englishwomen where the old gentleman had been and what he had done. They had no conception of its significance, but they did say, "Indeed?" and that began a conversation. The two ladies soon became Vi and Ann. And soon I was taking down their luggage, and saying good-by to the old gentleman. The train crossed a bridge and we were at Vaala. We got off, Ann and Vi and I, the chap from Chicago, and the girl who had sat alone in the corner.

We were at Vaala, but Vaala was no town, not even a station: the train stopped as soon as it crossed the bridge. On one side was the river and on the other a meadow. Across the meadow was the hotel which looked like a big country house.

Vaala was important to us, for it was to be the beginning of the adventure which was to shoot us through the rapids of the Oulu river in tar boats, cutting the waves and skirting whirlpools in a thrilling dash down to the sea. Shooting the Oulu rapids is a "must" on a tour of Finland, as important as Harry's American Bar to Paris, or Grant's Tomb to New York. And we were lucky, really lucky, because this was to be the last summer of shooting the Oulu rapids. Next year they were going to begin building a dam, and then a power plant that would put two hundred thousand horse-power to work. The Oulu will be left dry, and the bare rocks will stare at the sun.

We turned back to look at the Oulu, but it lay there behind the meadow like a quiet lake. Reeds were growing on the shore, and a rowboat floated placidly in the middle. There was no sound of churning water or angry waves, only the buzzing of mosquitoes.

Perhaps it was just as well to have this country solitude, this restfulness. Tomorrow we would be holding our breath: Vi would shriek, Ann would turn deadly pale, and our boat would head straight for a rocky shore. Perhaps it was just as well that the tourist association had arranged everything so that you arrived at Vaala in the afternoon but could not possibly shoot the rapids until the next noon. I arrived at the "philosophical" conclusion of the Americans who wrack their brains for five minutes over the knottiest of problems and then sigh cryptically, "It's just one of those things." I accepted the fact without five minutes' thought, for the food was excellent, and there was a *sauna* at the edge of the river, and coffee on the terrace at dusk, with the river looking like a nice, harmless lake.

But you could not miss the feeling of impending adventure. The unimpassioned account of an accident which I read in the morning newspaper remained in my thoughts: four lumberjacks were riding down the rapids; the oars broke; the boat careened; three of the men clung to the ruins and were saved, but the fourth one was lost. Jittery.

Ten minutes before starting time a bell sounds the shrill warning of a fire alarm. Your heart begins to beat faster, and you go down to the river to take your place, two on a seat, in the long tar boat, with a couple of boys at the bow holding long yellow oars, like huge pears on the end of a pole, an old man at the stern, calmly smoking a pipe and rubbing his unshaven chin. The old man counts. Twelve. A push —and we are off. No time for prayers now.

On the contrary, nothing happens. Nothing, unless you count the two boys seriously pulling the oars, thinking evil thoughts because they have to row twelve lazy tourists down the river, and it is a hard pull. Nothing, unless you count the motor boat crawling toward us: the man has a cap like a policeman's, but he turns out to be a mailman. Where are the rapids, and when is the excitement going to begin?

Somewhere the river has narrowed. The meadow has disappeared, and the trees creep ominously to the edge of the river. You hear the water rushing into the Niskakoski—the Neck Rapids. Here we go!

Seven kilometers of twists and bends, with the boat rolling, but not too much, the boys with their oars high in the air, Vi taking snapshots and not screaming at all. A slackening pace, much too soon. No, here we go again. You wave to those children on the shore. Isn't that a splendid farm? Crash—that was a wave—that girl behind you (the one who had sat alone in the train) got splashed. Another wave— and so was I.

I was much too wet. But Vi had not screamed, Ann was not pale, and nothing had happened except that I got wet. Then we had to leave the boat, climb a steep hill, buy some lukewarm orangeade from the woman with her table of bottles and glasses set up in the woods. Half a mile along a dusty path, then a half-hour wait for the train. I lay in the sun, trying to dry the seat of my trousers. I spread out the wet papers from my pocket—soaked travelers' checks, a letter from Berni with the ink running in blue streaks over the paper, a wet passport, stained blue around the edges. (I was not able to show that passport again without getting that look, and I could not very well say I had fallen into a river because I hadn't, but the blue edges were there just the same, and officials began to look at me twice, and thumb the passport very carefully.)

A half-hour train ride, another walk, then into the boat again. Twelve. Two boys and an old man. Another hard pull, and we began plunging down the Pyhäkoski—the Holy Rapids—the most thrilling part of the trip. Thrilling? There were no more wetting waves, just a few bumps, one moment when we headed straight for a cliff—and turned away at the last moment, just as Vi was about to scream. That was all. And because nervous tension like that makes you suddenly hungry, we stopped again, climbed up the cliffs, crossed a swaying suspension bridge to a restaurant pavilion in the woods. That was where the Oulu seemed its grandest: looking down from the high terrace at the river twisting down in its deep, cliff-lined gorge, with miles of forest everywhere, and only a coffee pavilion, a suspension bridge and our boat at the shore adding civilizing touches to the solitude. The river was dramatic. A few years ago you might have stood on this spot and seen the boats racing down to the sea—not with tourists, but with tar barrels, thousands of barrels a year, to be

sent to the corners of the world. Now logs race down
the river, and once a day a tar boat, gaily painted,
with pear-shaped oars, takes tourists down the river.
You must not miss Harry's American Bar, or Grant's
Tomb, or the Oulu river boat trip.

A "boat train" took us to the city of Oulu. It was
really an express, for we went by four stations without a halt. There is actually no reason for stopping
anywhere in this province of Ostrobothnia. It is vast,
flat, monotonous. We had gone around the Liminka
meadows, the rich sea-bottom lands devoted to sparse
grass, occasional ditches, and a few clusters of birch
trees. We had avoided the miles of plains that are
Finland's richest and least cultivated agricultural
lands. We had missed the people of Ostrobothnia
who survey their vast wealth and look dour. Thousands of them look menacingly dour: they are the
pietists, the "awakened" who wear black clothes and
avoid all worldly pleasures except meeting thousands
of other "awakened" souls at their big meetings every
summer. Up to a few decades ago, those who were
not "awakened" were either the Swedes, who fringe
along the coast of Ostrobothnia, or those puukko-
stabbing Finns who played at that gentle pastime for
the sheer joy it gave them.

Matti was one of the latter. It is not on record that
he ever stabbed anyone, but he might have done it if

he had had the chance. He was the youngest of four children, and surely the most dull-witted of them all. He was of no use at home, so he went into the world to seek his fortune, thinking that his great strength might be useful somewhere. He went all the way to the next village, which looked exactly like his own, and began to work for the blacksmith. His first task was to make the fire hotter, but he pushed the bellows so hard it burst with a moan and the fire kindled into bright, leaping flames.

"That won't do," the smith shook his head. "That won't do at all. Try something else: take that hammer and strike the anvil."

Matti lifted his hammer carefully and brought it down timidly on the anvil.

"No, Matti—strike harder, harder!"

Matti lifted his hammer high and brought it down swiftly and heavily on the anvil. It was a mighty blow, so strong that the anvil sank into the ground and completely out of sight.

"No, Matti—you won't do. You won't do at all. You had better go before I lose my patience altogether."

Matti went. The next day he was working for the village squire. He chopped down a few score trees, piled the logs high on the cart, and looked at the brown mare. She seemed to Matti the finest of horses, almost too good to pull a heavy load of wood. And even Matti confessed it was a heavy load. The mare pulled, pulled, pulled again. Slowly the cart began to move.

"Too slow," Matti decided. "We will have to think of something else." He unharnessed the horse, tied it to the back of the cart, and began to pull the heavy load of wood himself. A heave—a second heave, and they were on their way. Down through the woods they went, Matti pulling the cart, and the mare following lightly behind. Down the lane they went, and up to the squire's iron gates. There they stopped. The gateway was too narrow.

Matti sighed and began to pull harder. There was a crash, and the heavy iron gate posts gave way as Matti pulled the cart into the farmyard.

This was enough to frighten the squire and make his wife cry from fear: suppose something happened and Matti turned on them? In a council of war the squire and the servants determined that Matti must be gotten rid of: the next morning Matti was asked to dig a new well. Surely *he* could do it alone, the squire murmured.

Matti did not hesitate a moment. He began his task immediately, and by noon the hole was so deep that Matti looked like a little speck at the bottom. And still he kept on digging, trying hard to strike water.

There was a heavy millstone in the yard. The

frightened servants rolled the millstone quietly up to the very edge of the well that Matti was digging. Down went the millstone, and when the men peered into the well they saw the millstone draped just like a starched linen collar around Matti's neck. And very neatly it seemed to fit him, too.

"Heh," Matti shouted to the servants. "Where did you find my mother's old spinning wheel?" Then he went on calmly digging his well.

More frightened than ever, the servants ran to get the big bell from the church steeple. They carried the bell quietly into the farmyard, and with a loud cheer they dropped it into the well.

Matti grabbed the bell as it came down. He looked at it in amazement and cried out, "See here—where did you find my father's old Sunday hat?" He went on calmly digging until the well was finished.

Matti was just the man to fight the Russians, the squire decided, and sent him off to the wars.

Peter the Great discovered this Matti-like quality when he conquered Viipuri in 1710 and sent his armies to march across Finland. If victorious, the soldiers were to save as much of the land and people as possible; if in retreat, they were to destroy and burn property and enslave the people. The Russians were victorious enough: the Swedes retreated rapidly, and the only drawback was the stubborn, Matti-like resistance of the Finns. This resistance was so strong the Russians burned and pillaged, tortured and enslaved the Finns for an eight year period that went beyond war: it was annihilation.

This period of the Great Unrest was the beginning of the strong dislike for the Russians. If the Swedes of this period were not particularly able, they were not so bad as the Russians, who laid waste the cities, burned thousands of homes ("leaving nothing but the hearthstones, nought but in each yard the rowan"), slaughtered cattle and confiscated horses, carried off the men and women to Russia, conscripted the youth into Peter's armies. Those who were able escaped to Sweden. The rest wandered about as beggars, pillaged what was left, ate moss and bark, lived with the wolves in the forests. No crops were sown for years, and when attempts were made, the harvests failed. Disease and pestilence swept the land. There was neither law nor order, neither faith nor hope. It was "a day so dark the sun was not seen at noon, a night so cold the fire froze in the hearth." But after eight years, when half of Finland was destroyed and all of Ostrobothnia a wilderness, the Russians magnanimously made peace, even allowed Sweden to keep most of Finland—except Viipuri, which had not been destroyed.

Finland rose again as from the ashes, and remembered its bitterness. Ostrobothnia became rich again, but the people turned to pietism and have remained stolid and dour. The city of Oulu has prospered, but it is no gay Viipuri.

Oulu is memorable because here are the last of the rapids before the river pours into the sea, because Vi got gay, because we found ice cream there after a long harrowing search from café to café, because we had an excellent dinner. There was no hurry, no train waiting. We dismissed the boat trip as a disappointment. ("Clammily cool, that was it," I declared, remembering my wet trousers.) Vi whispered that the girl who had sat alone in the train was eating alone, two tables behind us. But we took some more reindeer meat and looked forward to Lapland.

Yes, of course there was a catch to it.

The train left at six-forty-five in the morning.

To sit all morning in a train, the rest of the day in a bus—was Lapland worth it?

"You know, it is actually disappointing," a German fellow confided to me in Helsinki. "Just tundra and rocky waste. *Mein Gott,* if I hadn't had colored film——"

"Lapland is marvelous," a Finnish novelist told me, with her big eyes rolled heavenward and her bosom heaving. "You will be enchanted."

A bank director shrugged his shoulders.

Lapland is a curious anomaly, for, like Valamo, it

is not Finland. At the same time it is Finland of another, a more northerly climate, a new frontier and new settlements, mineral wealth and the ice-free Arctic. For the tourist it is a corner of the North with Lapps and reindeer, tundra and rocky fells. Actually it is a vast, desolate domain north of the Arctic Circle. The home of a sad, stolid people who are called jealous, unforgiving, sly, but who are also good-hearted, hospitable, tender. A sad people who bow reverently before a cruel nature that does not permit the ground to thaw until June, that rushes flowers into blossom in July, ripens the berries in August, bids the birds and leaves desert the trees in September, and in October sends the snows. This nature relents to make the brief cycle of summer all the more intense in the mysterious day that is two months long. For two dramatic months the sun blazes across the sky day and night, with no pretense of sinking beyond the horizon:

> Yet mankind were all unknowing
> If the time was really morning,
> Or if perhaps it was still night-time.

What if the train did leave at a quarter to seven? We were satisfied with the prospect of adventure. Just the same, it was too bad the seats in the train were not wider, for that lonely girl sat by herself across the aisle, staring out of the window.

FINLAND

Not that there was much to see. There were no hills. The forests were lower; the trees, scrawny and starved. The hot sun poured through the windows and played with the choking dust that crept in through the double panes of glass.

I crossed the aisle to talk to the lonely girl.

She accepted a chocolate with quiet thanks but seemed happier when I offered her a cigarette. We were a gay party, weren't we? She was alone, but she had made up her mind to see something of Finland even if she did not have a companion. It was stupid to come all the way from America just to sit at home with her mother and father all summer at Ruovesi. What would her friends in New York say if she told them she had not traveled about? When I asked her about her home she told me how lovely it was, how her father looked after the Baron's fields, how she had spent a month lying on the sands of the lake. I knew the lake well; I had taken the steamer many times. Then I might even have seen her lying on the shore—if I remembered that sharp bend just before Ruovesi? Ah, it was a lovely place. How her friends in New York would envy her.

But why go to New York if it was so lovely in Ruovesi?

"Why?" she repeated, amazed at my question. "Why do any of us go to America? Don't you know?"

No.

"Money. That is what I went for." She compared herself to a girl who had dreamed of a little house with a garden. In America she had slaved making beds, cooking food and washing clothes until she had money enough to return to Finland to build the little house and plant the garden. Somehow the house seemed empty, the garden too quiet, and she went back to New York to make beds, cook food and wash clothes. "It is like a fever. I have come back before, twice, and each time I said to myself I would stay home, and marry, perhaps. But when the summer is over I go back to New York."

Poor girl—she looked like Aino might have looked if she had not drowned herself to escape the hero Wäinämöinen. Blond, with little wrinkles and shadows hovering around her blue eyes. Eyes that looked afraid because she had to go on, cleaning other people's houses, while she remembered how lovely it was to lie on the sand and greet that farmer's son (he was a neighbor) who came to drink a cup of coffee on Sunday afternoon. She was lost in the futile, never-ending whirl of going but not knowing where.

Lapland was an immediate goal. It would be something to tell friends about, proudly. But Rovaniemi—three miles from the Arctic Circle, farther north than Iceland, or the Yukon, or Archangel— is a pleasant city that does not look as it should.

143

FINLAND

There are no gleaming mountains of ice, no igloos, no polar bears, no reindeer, no Lapps. This capital of Lapland is a modern city. It boasts a super-modern hotel, but I heard no boasting about the sun—it blazed so hot we had to give up the idea of eating on the terrace and had our smorgasbord, reindeer meat and ice cream indoors. (Aino was too shy to join us.)

The mail bus to Petsamo was no better. There is always one person too many on each seat, and not half enough leg room. Then the heat—what a prospect: eight hours, and this on the Great Arctic Highway, the only road in the world to the icy sea! The three old maids from Philadelphia had turned up from somewhere and were planted in a row. They demanded air. A Danish family back of us pleaded for air. And because I was the only one who seemed to speak Finnish, I had to appeal to our driver to break a regulation if he must, but only give us air.

Three miles and stop, for "there is no hurry in Lapland" explains the native proverb. Everyone got out to look at the sign on the roadside: *Napapiiri*, Arctic Circle. There was no sudden change. The sun was still hot. Forests were still spread out on each side on the road, behind the ditches. Would it be like this for five hundred thirty-one kilometers? A straight level road, ditches, forest, hot sun? Stopping at every lonely mailbox to leave a newspaper and a household magazine with suggestions for an em-

broidered tablecloth, a crisp salad, and the latest
thing in beach clothes?

No, not quite. The background did change. Now
there were hills, now a lake ending in a swamp. Now
a stop for reasons of comfort, then the first town,
Sodankylä, with an area as large as two-fifths of Bel-
gium, but with only one main street—our Arctic
highway—lined with a few red houses, a yellow post
office, a gasoline pump, a restaurant of sorts, and
souvenir booths dealing in antlers, bone ornaments,
postcards and other useless junk.

Where were the Lapps? Centuries ago, when the
Finns came to Finland, there were Lapps everywhere. True, they had been chased north to Lapland,
but where were they hiding? Not one of the two
thousand Lapps stumbled upon the scene. It was
understandable reticence. As far back as a thousand
years ago the hunters and traders from Pirkkala
(near Tampere) penetrated northward to the Arctic.
These Pirkkala men claimed all trading rights with
the Lapps, bought furs from them for next to
nothing and then taxed them heavily in the bargain.
This "privilege" was not stopped until the sixteenth
century, and it was not until the seventeenth that the
Pirkkala men settled down to become good Ostro-
bothnian burghers, that the Lapps became Christians and settled down to herding their reindeer in
peace.

145

FINLAND

Aside from the fact that no one knows whence the Lapps came to Finland in the Stone Age, and what they are (besides looking Mongolian), the Lapp legend claims that before them there lived a still more ancient race in Finland. That was in those times before the god Jubmel upset the world in his anger.

When Jubmel turned the world upside-down the waters ran from the rivers and lakes and seas; the water covered the lands and drowned all the people except two children, a boy and a girl. Jubmel took these two children in his arms and carried them to a high mountain, Passevare, which was sacred to him. And when the waters had flowed back into the rivers and lakes and seas again, and there was no longer any danger, Jubmel set the two children free. They went gaily down the mountainside, and at the valley they separated and went in different directions, to the east and the west, to see if there were any other people living in the world.

Three years passed by before they met and recognized each other. They had seen no one so they separated once again and traveled three years more. They met and recognized each other, but after another three years they no longer knew each other, so they became man and wife, and from them all the Lapps are descended.

One of these descandants was Päiviö, rich in silver

146

and reindeer. He was a mighty warrior, but his three sons were even mightier. The eldest of them, Vuolabba, was so swift he could overtake a deer, so strong he could lift the rocks the giants found too heavy to carry. Once when the Russians came to wage war against Lapland, Vuolabba carried a huge log to the top of a mound and made the enemy believe his three-year-old son had done it. When Vuolabba's brother Isaac fought against the Russians he dined in the enemy camp. The Russian leader was clad in such heavy armor he could not eat without a servant lifting the fork to his mouth. Isaac ended the war by plunging the fork down the leader's throat. The third son, Juhani, was a mighty sorcerer, the like of whom we do not see today. When the Russians captured Juhani and forced him to guide them over the fells at night, he conjured the sound of bells and gleaming lights in the distance—and the Russians plunged over a cliff to their death.

At the moment, the only sorcery I could imagine was that of the mosquitoes. Someone had bewitched them into vicious black armies that came in angry droves to attack us. They crawled gingerly into one's hair, bit sharply through trousers, landed nonchalantly on noses. When we took a brisk walk, the mosquitoes followed still more briskly and drove us to St. Vitus antics. And they were not fooled when

FINLAND

Chicago and I took antlers from the souvenir booth at the next stop and placed them on our heads.

We had to admit it was an amateurish attempt when we saw the first reindeer. The little Danish boy had been on the look-out the whole trip, and while we were cursing mosquitoes he suddenly burst out with the news: a deer trotted gracefully across the road, his antlers high. In a moment there was not a trace of him, for his gray fur was as gray as the moss on the trees and rocks. All of us were as thrilled as the little boy, even the three old maids from Philadelphia, and we talked about it for five minutes as if it had been a miraculous sight, like a glimpse of the Holy Grail at the end of a pious life. We wondered when we would see the next one.

It was not a long wait. Two more deer crossed the road, giving us a blank stare before they wandered off. Another, a solitary chap. Then more and more, once a dozen all at once. What a wonderful place, this Lapland! And yet, the road was still monotonously straight, the ditches as deep, and kilometer-posts warned us we were not lost from civilization, even though the forest was still spread out in every direction. This forest served as the background of a solitary Lapp hut, half buried in the moss, with sloping walls and roof of poles, bunches of fir and moss. There was a mailbox in front of it.

Then the road began to slope up, the forest became thinner, and soon the firs disappeared altogether, leaving a few small white birches to fringe the tundra. But even the birches did not follow us to the heights of the Kaunispää fells. We had come half-way, and here at last was Lapland as I had imagined it. There were none of those sweeps of forest and lake that delight the heart further south. They had given way to desolate stretches of gray rocks and gray rocky hills sheltering a wisp of grass, a bit of dried moss, a crawling juniper bush. Lonely, an earth without form, and void. It leaves one bewildered, profoundly awed: as far as the eye carries— gray rock, emptiness, and the feeling that nothing has ever happened here. Nothing.

But I saw a Lapp. A young Lapp girl.

I had given up all hope, had deposited Ann and Vi and Chicago at the New Inn at Ivalo, with the Inari River flowing through the back yard and with the Danish fellow making love to his wife on the shore. Aino had joined us at coffee and had walked with me to the Old Inn at midnight. I sat down, dead tired, to write Berni a letter in that dim light of the oil lamp—and then, suddenly, I cursed letter writing, looked around, and there was the little Lapp girl, looking startled and afraid at the strange faces brooding in the shadows.

We were a motley crowd. There was only one bed

in all Ivalo where I could have slept the night, but it was behind so tightly closed windows I decided to go on to Liinahamari without sleeping. Now I was writing a letter, and making mistakes, while I waited for the bus to go on. Aino sat across the table, writing postcards to her friends in America. She was alone; might she come along with me? A Frenchman stared at us from across the room—he was equipped with knickers that billowed almost to his ankles, a tropical helmet of pressed cardboard, a horrible beard, a black umbrella and a knapsack. Two tired, unshaven fishermen were discussing a murder, a wild chase, and two detectives sleeping in a cabin behind the inn. A little puppy in a covered box near the window cried and whined in its loneliness. The little Lapp girl turned her eyes away. I gloated over my good luck.

There are only two reindeer and one-fiftieth of a Lapp to a square kilometer in Lapland. Still more important, in this day when Lapps (as well as bootleggers, artists, and the girls at Woolworth's) are beginning to look like respectable people anywhere, to live in houses, to read newspapers and a magazine with directions for making an embroidered tablecloth and a crisp salad, my Lapp girl was still dressed in the vivid blue, embroidered tunic of the Lapps, and was wearing the four-wind hat.

When northward-penetrating colonization and the

taxes of the Pirkkala men drove these people into
Lapland, their drama of life against nature became
an elemental one. Keeping reindeer was the accepted
livelihood, for the deer furnished their keepers with
food and shelter, warmth, tools and transportation.
As long as the herds stayed together, as long as they
were not molested by wolves, the Lapp was happy
and rich. In the spring he moved to the Arctic
shores to fish, and in the summer months he fished in
his own ponds and slept in his tent. In the winter
he joined the few families that constituted his tribe
and his village, counted his reindeer, settled his affairs, traded, got married, and was taxed.

Nowadays the Lapp can be classed as an Inari
Lapp, whose father already lived in a house; he fishes
and keeps reindeer, but he also cultivates a potato
patch. Or he may be a Skolt-Lapp, Greek Orthodox
and Russian, who does not understand the language
of the other Lapps. Or he may be one of the two
hundred wandering, pure-blooded "tundra" Lapps
who has a home for the winter, but who still herds
his reindeer, avoids the mobs of curious tourists,
lives the life of his fathers, and wears the hat of the
four winds—like my Lapp girl.

Her small eyes were wide open, her graceful hands
restless. She looked frightened in that rough room
in the inn—in the thick smoke that made the oil
lamp still more useless, in the din of the heavy coffee

cups banging on the bare tables, the voices of the motley crowd, the whining of the puppy—and she longed for the tundra and the birches and her father's tent on the edge of a lake. It was a moment to remember.

Of the trip to Liinahamari, of that night in the bus, I remember nothing except that the bus jolted along through the twilight-dawn, with an occasional glimpse of a reindeer, or a lake with a fisherman, or a gasoline pump. The Frenchman sat upright with the tropical helmet on his head, while Aino slept in one corner and I in another. When we stopped I would wake up with a start, drink a cup of bitter coffee, fall asleep again. Once we came to a river where hundreds of men were busy building a dam to capture the rapids. The heavy trucks and the machines pouring out concrete drowned out the dull roar of the rapids. The Canadians needed power to blast the nickel from Petsamo's rocky hillsides.

Petsamo is essentially a narrow corridor to the Arctic which everyone has claimed. All Scandinavia claimed it and fought for it because of the excellent fishing waters. The Russian Tsars needed it on imperial grounds and because it furnished their annual supply of arctic berries. Even a British force occupied Petsamo for a while. Twenty years ago, by the treaty of Dorpat, Petsamo became Finnish, the Russians "reserving only the right to cross the province should military exigencies require." It was essential to the Finnish cartographers to have Petsamo, for how would the ladylike form of Finland look with only one arm?

The bus jolted along. There may have been more gasoline pumps and nickel mines, a Lapp settlement and a Russian monastery, but when I opened my eyes we were at Liinahamari. We washed our faces, Aino and I, had coffee, and were ready for the Arctic Ocean.

It eluded us. It should have been there at Liinahamari, three hundred and twenty-five miles north of the Arctic Circle, but it was not. Liinahamari is Petsamo's ice-free port, deep in a fiord, surrounded by bald gray summits of rock. Near one corner of the harbor is the tourist inn, aloof and by itself. The Great Arctic Highway goes on for another half mile, past a co-operative store, a wharf, a few houses, a fish-meal factory, a tavern, another wharf. Mention might still be made of a few birch trees, some birds, and a couple of tramp steamers. One of them looked rusty and deserted, but the other was busily discharging bags of concrete. When we passed this latter steamer in the afternoon, everything was quiet. The captain's wife had hung her laundry on the deck, and the wharf had been scrubbed clean. The scene of activity had shifted to the tavern, where the sailors were loudly rejoicing to the strains of an accordion.

But I had not spent two days in a train and a day and a night in a bus just to see a harbor with a couple of tramp steamers and hear the carousing sounds typical of any sailors' dive. I had come—well, expecting something entirely strange. Not that I had colored film in my camera, or usually rolled my eyes heavenward in ecstatic gestures, but I did not want to go back and—shrug my shoulders, as if to say that it was all well and good if you wanted to see a few reindeer and gray rocks and did not mind mosquitoes or interminable bus rides.

A clerk at the inn told us it was only eight kilometers to the Arctic. It turned out to be fifteen, but it was not too long. The wind-espaliered birches followed us on the steep path up the mountainside. Below us lay Liinahamari at the edge of its fiord: not like those of Norway which I vaguely remember as a strip of peaceful meadow, a red cottage and a couple of cows at the foot of sheer walls of forbidding rock, Liinahamari's fiord was a blue scroll of water, surrounded by old gray hills touched with purple, a warm sun and a dazzling clear sky. As soon as we lost the fiord we lost the birches, and were suddenly left on the edge of an Alpine meadow of coarse grass dotted with cheerful white flowers. Now we crept along a narrow ledge which bordered a crater lake, now we jumped from rock to rock. We were walking through the gray wilderness of rocks and lonely tarns that is the top of the world. Then came the moment when we could look down and see the meadow of rock sloping down to a strip of white sand and sea, the open sea which stretched out to meet the sky.

As I rode back to Rovaniemi through the monotony of a straight road, two ditches and a forest of moss and fir, I could not forget this wilderness of rock and sea. It was as if I had suddenly awakened in the cold dawn but forgotten my dream, had groped vainly for it only to feel that the earth was without form, and void; that life was nothing; that there was no life, no significance—and had gone on living, remembering the wind-espaliered birches, remembering the white meadow flowers and the Lapp girl. And the long bus ride back to Rovaniemi.

WHITE CITY OF THE NORTH

HELSINKI'S MARKET-PLACE is lined with little palaces on one side and the South Harbor on the other. At one edge of this square, where the broad Esplanade comes to an abrupt stop, is a fountain. Four seals curve their necks to spout up water at the figure on the high pedestal. It is the statue of a well-rounded lady who seems to be lost in meditation. She has been swimming and looks quite sparkling and fresh in the sun. Her towel hangs limply over one leg as she looks at the harbor with a wondering gaze. The natives are on good terms with the lady and call her "Havis Manda," but actually she is Helsinki rising from the sea.

That is the way to see Helsinki first: rising from the sea. As the ship sails northward on the Baltic, the atmosphere becomes more and more unreal. The sun sinks reluctantly, leaving the sky pink all night; a red half-moon appears for a while but gives up the struggle as the sun, after a five-hour rest, appears with new vigor. The water seems a deeper blue under the vivacious sky. There is no movement, no noise but the soft steady beat of the engines and the occasional faint swish of water foaming at the stern. A few rocks appear, then larger ones with five or six

FINLAND

squat pine trees and a patch of grass. Now, too numerous to count, they spread everywhere, and the white ship slips by a fortress—pink granite should not be used, it cannot manage to look forbidding. Behind the fortress comes a blue bay—the South Harbor—and in the background, with the fleecy clouds pointing to it, the dazzling white city of Helsinki rises slowly over the horizon. The boat creeps closer, until it is almost in the center of the city. If the Swedish minister, or the mayor, or the president of Finland looked out of their windows they could see you marching down the gangplank. You walk a few steps along the cobblestone quay and come face to face with a young lady on a pedestal looking at you with a wondering gaze.

Helsinki began life four hundred years ago, but her oldest buildings are only a hundred years old. For centuries she has been a sleeping princess, but a few decades ago she woke up, spread over the granite hillsides and meadows to become the white city of the North. In 1550 the energetic Gustav Vasa had decided to found this city on the south coast of Finland, with the idea of making it the Finnish trade center and a curb to Hanseatic domination in the Baltic. The burghers of the old coastal cities, Rauma and Porvoo and a few others, were given the privilege of settling in Helsinki. The burghers were reluctant. They were seriously spoken to, afforded a good start and many advantages if they would move. The burghers were still reluctant. Gustav was determined that Helsinki should flourish and threatened the burghers with a death penalty if they did not move. The gentle coercion worked; Helsinki was settled. However, when Gustav Vasa looked at his handiwork a few years later, it looked so hopeless that he gave the burghers permission to go back home. They marched eagerly back to Rauma and Porvoo, and Helsinki was left to fade into an insignificant village.

Helsinki was not heard of again until Gustav Adolph called together a Finnish Diet to meet him in Helsinki in 1616. For ten days the representatives of the nobility and the church, soldiers and landowners met to hear about the schemings of Sigismund of Poland and the threat of Russian attacks, both of which could be dealt with by a war tax. The Finns imposed the tax on themselves, especially since Gustav patiently listened to their grievances and took a hand in settling farmers' disputes.

Again Helsinki was not heard of until Peter the Great aroused the Great Unrest of Finland. Helsinki was swept by epidemic, and in 1713, when Peter sailed into the South Harbor with several hundred ships and twelve thousand men, the Finnish garrison of fifteen hundred could do no more than retreat, after burning the city to a pile of ashes. Instead of leaving it in such a state, Peter realized the great strategic significance of the location and built a high wall around the pile of ashes, strengthened it with numerous batteries and a few fortifications on the islands at the mouth of the harbor. After the war the Finns saw the value of the defenses Peter had built, and work was begun on the Viapori fortress in the harbor. The work was carried on for decades, with the result that the fortress was soon known as the northern Gibraltar and the most impregnable fortress in all Europe.

In 1808, after Napoleon had sold out Finland to Russia and Alexander had finally invaded the land, Klingspor retreated with the Finnish army as rapidly as possible to the north. The Russian army headed straight for Helsinki and found quantities of arms and ammunition, destined for the Viapori fortress, carelessly left about in the city. They seized the arms and began to bombard Viapori.

The commander of the fortress, Admiral Cronstedt, was cut after the same pattern as the weak-kneed Klingspor: Klingspor had fled, King Gustav was ready to give up Finland, so the cowardly Cronstedt asked himself why he should fight. Sweden could not control the land much longer—would it not be better to give in? When the Russians suggested that Viapori cannon should not bombard Helsinki—it was a shame to destroy so fine a city—Cronstedt agreed, and the Russians picked themselves attractive and safe quarters in the city and began a comfortable and leisurely bombardment of the fortress from the neighboring hilltops. It did not amount to much; Viapori would never fall with such maneuvers. (It need not have surrendered: in 1855, during the Crimean War, the combined English and French fleets bombarded Viapori for two days and two nights: nothing happened: Viapori was still intact, and the English and French sailed away in disgust.) Then the Russians began to talk to Cronstedt: they admitted to him that the Russian forces were unlimited; they assured him the Finnish soldiers in the north were prisoners to the last man; they convinced him that there had been a revolution in Sweden, that French soldiers marched on the streets of Stockholm. The Russians fostered these reports with well-placed bribes, and Cronstedt believed everything. He made a hasty agreement with the Russians.

First of all, they would have a month's truce, to the beginning of May. If at least five Swedish boats did not sail into the harbor within this time, Viapori would be given over to the Russians. Cronstedt did not really believe the ships would arrive: the harbor was frozen, and he had included provisions in the truce for marching his men across the ice to safety. Next, Cronstedt gave the Russians three of the northern fortifications in the Viapori chain, one of them outright, the other two to be returned to the Finns if the ships should come!

The ships did not appear. Cronstedt quelled a revolt among his rebellious Finns, and in May he marched his men out of the fortress—over the ice—leaving the Russians more than a hundred ships, two thousand cannon, thousands of rifles, plenty of ammunition and six thousand prisoners. Viapori was Russian; the gate and stronghold of Finland was captured. This was at the beginning of the war, but the Russians considered the war already won. A *Te Deum* was sung in St. Petersburg, and a long parade marched around the statue of Peter the Great.

Four years later Helsinki became the new capital of Finland. It had a better location than Turku, it was not as far from St. Petersburg, it had a harbor big enough to hold all the Baltic fleets at once, and it was not steeped in Swedish tradition like ancient Turku. A Berlin architect, Carl Ludwig Engel, who had fled from war-torn Prussia to design buildings in St. Petersburg, was called to Helsinki to make a city worthy of being called the capital of Finland. For three decades Engel worked in Helsinki, designing churches and barracks, palaces and government buildings, stables and summerhouses. His achievement is noteworthy: the earliest spirit of present-day Helsinki is Engel's, and the best manifestation of this spirit is the monumental Suurtori, the Big Square.

This square is the heart of the old city. It is bordered with buildings of severe, neo-classic lines that housed the life of Finland with equal severeness. The big State Council building—it had to be a big building, for the bureaucratic government needed almost as many officials as people whose private lives had to be supervised—rises along the eastern edge, symbolic, perhaps, in that Russia lay to the east. Directly opposite the State Council building stands the University, at the western side of the square, and though it was called the Royal Alexander University and had to restrict its academic freedom, the academic tradition was certainly western and concerned itself with authoritative discussions in Swedish and Latin of the problems of law and religion and medicine. The Big Church (it used to be called the Nicholas Church) towers over the square from the north. It rests on a terrace above a long broad flight of stairs and looms high above the other buildings of the city. With the little cupolas added to the church after Engel's death, this church might look a bit Russian to someone seeking to claim that maybe the Finns are a bit Russian, after all, but it is nothing more than a misguided Byzantine onion breath on an otherwise classical building. The Italians would not call it strange if it stood opposite St.

Peter's. In any event, the church stands on the north, and represents that northern, coldly intellectual religion which is as pure as a glass of water. To complete the quadrangle, the southern side has three streets leading to the South Harbor, and in the narrow spaces between the streets are the police headquarters, municipal offices and courts. There are no policemen directing traffic, for today it is a quiet square, and you can walk crisscross over the cobbled paving and stand where you please. There are no trees, no fountains, but there is a statue of Alexander II, put there by the Finns. In this square, and around this statue, a century of Finnish history has revolved.

Alexander I, Finland's first Russian Grand Duke, was a peculiar man, combining such contradictory traits as love of liberty and a taste for military exploits. The desire to be a great military figure compelled him to conquer Finland. His belief in "the sacred rights of humanity" then urged him to promise Finland at a solemn meeting of its parliament a "political existence," the preservation of its religion, laws and liberties. He soon forgot his liberal ideas and his benevolent attitude, because he had neither the patience nor the strength to go through with any program either at home or in his new Grand Duchy. He did nothing much for or against Finland. The memorable events of his reign included making Helsinki the capital, declaring Tampere a city, and traveling hurriedly through rural Finland. Thus Alexander can be credited with giving shape to Helsinki's Big Square, having vision enough to imagine the village of Tampere a city, and making his trip through rural Finland notable because he ate a meal in somebody's stable.

With a new tsar the Finns had to swear allegiance to a new monarch, and he in turn dutifully promised to respect Finland's rights. However, Nicholas I was not like his older brother Alexander had been. While Alexander had been studying law books and dreaming over Rousseau, Nicholas had played war games, had learned to be hard, had learned to trust no one but himself. He believed in "discipline" and applied it thoroughly and successfully for thirty years, long enough to acquire the title of the "Iron Tsar," long enough to break his heart when this discipline failed him miserably in the Crimean War. When the Finns tactfully suggested they would like a meeting of their parliament, Nicholas replied curtly that "at this time the conditions, and his other cares and duties, did not permit him to call the Finnish Diet." These other cares and duties included the introduction of a severe censorship on all literature except printed sermons and a codification of Finnish law, with the purpose of making room for laws more congenial to the Russians. Just at the moment when Lönnrot brought forth the evidence of

FINLAND

Finland's culture in the *Kalevala,* Runeberg expressed the Finns' indomitable patriotism in the *Songs of Ensign Stål,* and Snellman urged the Finns to speak Finnish and thus be real Finns, Nicholas determined that Finland should not be Finland at all but Russia.

1855 brought a new tsar and an oath of allegiance to a new monarch. It brought a promise by Alexander II to respect Finland's religion, laws and institutions—and a surprise to the Finns because he stuck to the promise. As soon as he concluded peace with England, Alexander went to Helsinki, called the Diet together for the first time in forty-five years and ordered the Finnish legislators to foster commerce and shipping, build factories, improve communications, advance education, and raise wages. Hopes of a constitutional government for Finland immediately awakened again. Alexander opened the Diet with a speech in French; Snellman countered with his "Speech Manifesto" in Swedish, giving the Finnish language an equal footing with the Swedish in the government, the courts and public institutions. The censorship against printed matter was lifted, schools were established, Swedish kröner and Russian rubles were replaced by Finnish marks, roads were built, a railroad begun.

Alexander was known as the great reformer Tsar. Although he did nothing as spectacular for Finland as he did at home in freeing Russia's forty million serfs, Finland thrived under his rule. It could be called a spectacular thriving in comparison to Poland's fate: the Poles attempted a revolt, whereupon Poland lost her language, her church its wealth, her nobility its power. With this Polish revolt Alexander's reforming zeal vanished, but in Finland the provincial officials were commanded to use Finnish. A law was passed, and approved by Alexander, calling for a parliament every five years. The franchise was extended. A new church law was passed, taking education out of the hands of the church and lessening state control over the church itself. In Russia, however, anarchists, nihilists and terrorists began to temper autocracy with assassination. Alexander was one of their victims.

The cause of despotism was bolstered. Alexander III announced that he was going to avenge his father's murder, that he was going to be as autocratic, ruthless and reactionary as he pleased. Russia was going to be Russia, Holy Russia, and not an imitation of a liberal, democratic, western European nation. For a time things still went well in Finland, but soon Finland's progress was declared not in harmony with Russia's spirit. The nominal independence of Finland as a Grand Duchy, with its own laws and institutions, became a thorn in the side of the Russian conservatives and bureaucrats. The forgotten censorship was brought out again; the postal system was joined to Russia's; the Finnish constitution was looked on as dangerous.

In 1894 the Finns erected a monument in the Big Square, in front of the cathedral: it was a statue of Alexander II surrounded by symbolical groups of peace, art and science, labor, and law—Finland defending her constitution. It was raised in gratitude to a Tsar who had honored Finland's laws, raised as a reproach to Alexander III, who showed no signs of honoring Finland's laws.

Alexander III did not have time to meditate on the silent reproach, for he died that year, and his son, Nicholas II, followed in his father's footsteps by ignoring any symbolism the statue might have, and by ushering in Finland's darkest days. He began with a proposal which was to place Finnish military service on the same plane as Russia's. He hurried on to the "February Manifesto" of 1899 which drastically curtailed Finland's constitution: the emperor was to decide all matters of "imperial" interest; the Russian Duma, lesser matters; the Finish Diet, minor matters.

In eleven days over five hundred thousand Finns appealed to the emperor's conscience by signing a petition, rapidly and secretly circulated in the snowbound Finnish midwinter through all towns, villages and backwoods farms, even beyond the Arctic

Circle. In the middle of March five hundred men went to St. Petersburg to present the petition to Nicholas. Nicholas refused to see them. All Europe became interested, and men like Zola and Anatole France, Ibsen and Mommsen, signed an address. Six men were delegated to bring it to Nicholas. Nicholas refused to see them. He was not one whit daunted in his program. He made Russian the official language of Finland, he forbade public meetings, he dissolved the Finnish army and demanded Finnish recruits to report in St. Petersburg.

The Finns began an organized, passive resistance. The recruits failed to report to the military authorities.

A "dictator decree" was planned to break this passive resistance: Governor-General Bobrikov became all-powerful and was allowed to use whatever means he chose in his care for "the quiet of the land." Judges were arrested; provincial governors were arrested. Houses were searched. Anyone was liable to arrest—and exile in Siberia.

In those dark days a motto hung on the walls of most Finnish homes: "A new day can still change everything." It was a ray of hope from Runeberg's *Ensign Stål*. In most homes there was also a crude colored lithograph, sometimes hidden in the bottom of a trunk or under the wallpaper, in attics or outhouses: a picture of Finland holding a tablet *LEX* close to her bosom, while the Russian double eagle pounced, trying to shatter the tablet. Having this picture in your possession was cause enough for a winter in Siberia. In most Finnish hearts there was the belief that officials "do not die a proper death: they can never be blessed."

General Bobrikov made Russian obligatory in the schools. The Finnish customs and financial setups were about to be abolished. The Russifying of the legal system was being studied. Then, in June, 1904, Eugen Schaumann killed General Bobrikov.

Eugen Schaumann was a twenty-eight-year-old minor official in the educational bureau at Helsinki. He was shy, hard of hearing. He liked hunting, he loved the *Songs of Ensign Stål*. One June morning he put a letter in his pocket, shot Bobrikov as he was coming out of the State Council Building, and killed himself a moment later. The letter in his pocket was addressed to the Tsar: it was necessary to kill Bobrikov and himself, Schaumann declared, as the means of letting the emperor know the extent of the unrest and dissatisfaction in Finland. The Finns sighed with relief and gave Schaumann a hero's burial in Porvoo, near the grave of his idol Runeberg.

Nicholas might have countered with some polite gesture, like planting a row of trees in the Big Square. As it is, the sun blazes into the square with full fury. There is no relief in sight, for the only things you can buy are flowers, which are no help at all, and ice cream, which is hardly better. You leave the square, but Alexander Street does not help much, for it is bent on continuing the square's dignity and impressiveness with gray granite buildings and pink granite buildings, with banks and offices and shops. You turn into the huge Railway Square, so impressive that you go out of your way, whenever possible, just to see it. Again there are flower and ice-cream stands, of course, but also cigarette and newspaper kiosks, for here is a square that lives today. It is as vast as Engel's square, but Engel's Helsinki might as well be a hundred miles away as only five minutes distant.

There are nondescript buildings on one side of the Railway Square; the art galleries of the Atheneum on another, in a shabby renaissance building, badly in need of being torn down; opposite the Atheneum the National Theater, drab gray, trying not to look classical or renaissance and failing to look Finnish. Disappointing in themselves, these buildings do not matter, for they serve merely as foils for Eliel Saarinen's railroad station. You can comb the world for a finer station to compare it to, and then perhaps discover the one in Viipuri—which Saarinen also designed. Warm pink granite, with arched copper roofs, the building stretches this way and that to fill half the square and more. It is vertical in spirit, with tall windows and a glorious tower. It is rounded, too, with a gracefully arched portal flanked by stone genii holding lamps. Begun before Finland gained her independence, if Nicholas had possessed any architectural awareness he would surely have halted this building before it was started as contrary to the Russian spirit—for you cannot imagine anything more intensely Finnish than the Helsinki railroad station in material, imagination, design or decoration. Nicholas was too busy. Holy Russia was showing signs of unrest.

In 1905, on the heels of the disastrous war with Japan, a general strike broke out throughout Russia. The emperor capitulated and declared Russia a constitutional monarchy on the thirtieth of October. On that same day the Finns gathered in a mass meeting in the Railway Square to proclaim a general strike for Finland, the senate appealed for the removal of the "dictator decree," and the masses clamored for a wider franchise and a new constitution. The strike began: for a week life was at a standstill. Then Nicholas listened: he removed the hated decree and the February Manifesto, he restored the old laws and liberties.

"The present moment is a historical turning point," declared the Finns, "which challenges all the power in the state to the creation of a brighter future for the fatherland." By the following February a new constitution was ready, establishing a pure democracy, giving everybody over the age of twenty-four, men and women alike, the right to vote. The next step was independence.

The outbreak of European war in 1914 brought the old restrictions back to Finland. That was nothing unusual. But in 1917 Nicholas abdicated—the tsars had held Finland to Russia, but now that the tsars were gone, did it mean independence for Finland?

No. The old restrictions were merely removed once more; Kerensky ordered a session of the Diet, but curtly suggested that activities be limited to those previously granted. Kerensky gave way to Lenin, and on December 6, 1917, the Finns proclaimed Finland a sovereign state.

If you go past the pink granite station; then past the new yellow brick post office which looks like two match boxes, one on end and the other lying flat—it is labeled "Posti" but the Swedes also want the sign "Post," which means the same thing in Swedish; then across the street, still cobblestone, you will see a granite knoll with the magnificent building the Finns have erected as a symbol of their independence: the new parliament building, of light reddish-gray granite, dignified, new yet ageless, with an Egyptian base topped with a row of Roman columns.

FINLAND

The huge round session chamber is the focal point, of course. Here the representatives of seven parties, two hundred men and women—farmers and teachers, business men and nurses, woodcutters and mail carriers—make laws and speak speeches. The speeches are usually in Finnish, though if you want to, you may also speak in Swedish. It is a decorative room, with statues in tall slender niches behind the speaker's desk: mental work on the left, wiping his brow or shading his eye from too much light all at once; faith next to him, looking at something—it could be a mirror—in his palm; the pioneer at the right, looking careworn, and the harvester, looking satisfied; the future in the middle: a woman with her back turned, holding in her arms an infant who casts a parting glance and waves good-by to the assembled legislators.

You can survey a century of history in the Big Square, come and go from the Railroad Square and the pink station building, or wonder how much the lawmakers' attention is focused on the future, a woman's turned back and a babe in arms, but that is not of vital importance in any city. You can take ten Turku cathedrals and castles if you will let me keep Viipuri's Torkel. You can take the Big Square and any number of legislative chambers if you will give me Helsinki's Esplanade, the heart of the white

city of the North. There is life and significance in
Helsinki. Lapland fades rapidly from memory as
a dream of rocky fells and nightless, sleepless nights;
Valamo seems like something that has no place in
this world. In Turku today may be as yesterday, but
on Helsinki's Esplanade you live today and look
eagerly toward tomorrow.

The Esplanade is a gay double boulevard, with a
band of park in the middle. It stretches from the
Swedish opera house, with the restaurant terraces
and Strauss waltzes of the Royal in its backyard; to
the Kappeli, a restaurant with terraces, a glass building for rainy weather, and more Strauss waltzes;
meets Helsinki (or Havis Manda) rising from the
sea, and empties into the market-place skirting the
South Harbor. The buildings of this double boulevard house movies, restaurants, fashionable hotels
and night clubs, cocktail lounges and milk bars.
Here gloomy history and foreboding future are forgotten in the brightness and fulfillment of the moment.

The Esplanade is never deserted. Sometime during the day or night everybody in Helsinki strolls
through the tree-shaded, music-filled Esplanade.
Babies and nurse-maids take their turn, then young
men with canes and portly gentlemen with dogs on
leashes, followed by business men who know that
time is money, and women who do not get up until

the afternoon. Thrifty housewives pretending to hurry home, with flowers and vegetables from the market-place under their arm, schoolboys, smart automobiles, droshkies, diplomats and tourists. An army band on parade, soldiers on parade, soldiers in ones and twos. Two soldiers nonchalantly eating ice-cream cones as they stroll along. They seem like boys fresh from school, these soldiers, looking wistfully at the posters in front of the movie houses, with the sign *Soldiers and children, half-price* in the ticket window. They look still more wistful in their barracks: when you walk past (it is not far from the Esplanade) you can see them leaning out of the windows, looking over the roof-tops at the sky, smoking a cigarette, listening to a concertina, and telling the other fellow about home, a cottage on the edge of a lake. Soldiers and children half-price. . . .

In the middle of the Esplanade is a statue of Runeberg as a dignified, middle-aged gentleman in a Prince Albert coat. Artistically, it is not exciting, but he stands here in a pose that makes him look as if he owned the Esplanade and a lot more, besides. It was probably put here to compensate Runeberg a bit for having to forgo the pleasures of Helsinki.

When Turku University moved to Helsinki, Runeberg came along as docent in Latin. In time he might have become a full professor but for an incident, trivial in itself but disastrous in the Helsinki of a century ago. A few young instructors and a group of excited undergraduates who had just passed their examinations went to a café to celebrate. The punch was good. So good that it was not long before one of the company was indiscreet enough to lift his glass in a toast to Poland, which had just begun another of its rebellions against Russian rule. The chap was soon silenced; it was determined to keep the incident secret. There was only one person they were not quite sure of—a mathematics docent who had just slid under the table. Was he aware of what had happened?

A few months later, after Runeberg had just married, the mathematics docent went to the Governor-General. Runeberg had once exuberantly bounced a snowball against the silk topper of the serious docent, and now the docent told the Governor-General that Runeberg had drunk a toast to Poland. The Governor-General told Nicholas I, and Nicholas ordered everyone who had been connected with the affair to join the Russian army—as soldiers in the ranks. This fate was averted at the last moment, but Runeberg's advancement at the University was blocked—there was no room for radicals or revolutionaries. Runeberg resigned. He found a position teaching Latin at the secondary school in Porvoo, and left Helsinki for good.

He did not have far to go, for Porvoo is quite near

FINLAND

Helsinki: two hours by train or four hours by boat. Runeberg went by land, which is a strange choice, especially for a poet. I tried both, and the boat is by far the better. It leaves from the South Harbor, just like an important vessel, and bounces down the bay. As soon as it is out of sight of the city, however, it clings to the narrow channels between the islands and the curling coastline:

> Wheresoe'er her hand she pointed,
> There she formed the jutting headlands;
> When toward the land she turned her,
> There the level shores extended;
> Where her head the land touched lightly,
> There the curving bays extended.

Eventually, after innumerable stops at the piers of red villas with a backdrop of green forest, the steamer glides up a narrow river and comes to a stop at Porvoo. Porvoo used to be a trading center, with a church on one hill-top and a castle on another, just like a village on the Rhine—complete to the robber baron who used to dash down from his hill-top to raid the rich burghers. The city has been burned and plundered and laid waste time and again. Finally the castle disappeared, the city walls were torn down, and Porvoo gave up all thoughts of trade. Now it advertises only its picturesqueness. It is picturesque: each time the city burned down the burghers only shrugged their shoulders and proceeded to rebuild in the old pattern, down the steep slopes of the hill crowned with the old stone church, their only concession a few inches more width to the cobweb-patterned streets—say an increase from five and a half feet to six. Everyone was contented, but when Nicholas I visited the city a century ago, he horrified Porvoo by suggesting it should grow. He called in Engel to solve the problem: the result is a "new" quarter in neo-classic style on what used to be a meadow at the edge of the river below the city. Here the streets are straight and wide; they meet each other at right angles, and the houses stretch out in long, monotonous rows, carefully hiding their gardens in back.

It is to this city that Runeberg came, arriving on a dark, rainy midnight. He did not like it at first, but it slowly came to mean "home" to him, and he stayed forty years, except for summers in the country and one trip to Stockholm to receive Swedish adulation. He lived in a house in the "new" quarter, and every day for twenty years he walked up the hill, winding through the cobblestone streets to the *gymnasium* behind the church. The last twenty years he spent in retirement, confined to his home. Every year on Runeberg's birthday his house is brightly lighted, flares burn outside, and a procession of citizens with lighted torches marches to his grave.

FINLAND

His home has become a shrine. Finnish admirers say it had "artless simplicity and harmony which is full of sentiment." I say it is a faded pumpkin yellow house in a wild, overgrown weed-bed called a garden. In the hall his moth-eaten brown felt hat still hangs on a peg, and his walking-stick leans against a corner. The house is full of palms, red walls, red plush, red damask, embroidered cushions sent by blushing young admirers, romantic paintings (Storm at Sea, Rocky Beach, Mountainous Landscape with Fiord, Fallen Warrior) and plaster casts (Narcissus, Goethe, Runeberg). More red plush. . . .

I took the next train back to Helsinki.

I went straight to the Esplanade, but I avoided the statue of a dignified chap in a Prince Albert. There were plenty of other statues around: two slim girls standing on tiptoe; the three naked smiths pounding their anvil; coffee and Strauss waltzes at the Kappeli, in full view of the fountains playing on Helsinki rising from the waves in what is the most marvelous of market-places.

I never got up early enough to beat the farmers to the market-place—when I got there business was always in full swing: booths with vegetables and fruits, booths with meats, piles of baskets and boxes, on one edge the fish vendors in their boats, on the other, flower stalls in a decorative fringe. It is hard to walk nonchalantly past, past the stalls in front of

the Swedish embassy, past the obelisk (the Empress
Alexandra Feodorovna stepped on shore here in
1833, so someone commemorated the event with an
obelisk), past the president's palace, to the Greek
church, magnificently located on a rocky summit.
The church is a mass of red brick, tortured curves,
a tin roof dully gray, and gilt onions topped with
tarnished crosses.

The building is unimportant now, and ugly ware-
houses have crept up to its very feet. It is still worth
the climb, for the view is glorious. The city spreads
out below you: there is the Big Church proud on
another height—white and restrained, the broad
Esplanade and the market-place, the harbor, the
jagged shore and scattered islands. What a marvelous
city, with islands enough to be able to give one to a
zoo; another to an outdoor museum with old houses
and barns, a church and even a cemetery, trans-
planted there from all over Finland; one to a fashionable suburb; and islands enough so that plenty
of them can be left to rocks and firs. Rocky promon-
tories where people can sun themselves and look at
the city they have created: modern white apartment
houses for everyone, rich and poor alike; breath-
taking hospitals and schools; parks. These people
have Europe's largest bookstore—and they throng it
from morning until closing time. They have a vast
stadium and fill it with crowds cheering the prow-

ess of their athletes. They still keep their *saunas,* and shop in the market-place, but they have restaurants that seat a thousand, a night club that seats fifteen hundred, fashionable restaurants with superb food piled on gargantuan tables, restaurants on rooftops and in towers—Mitchell was sure he could feel the perfume of pine trees even on the fourteenth-floor roof garden restaurant of the Torni—but then, Mitchell was English, and I agreed politely and suggested we see the daily ritual that transforms the market-place.

At noon the booths fold up; in ten minutes they are all gone. A truck gathers the boxes and papers that are left; women appear with brooms; a sprinkler truck rolls back and forth. At twelve-thirty the square is washed clean, and the flower vendors linger on near Havis Manda: the white steamers are still anchored in the harbor; perhaps someone will want flowers when he sails. The flower carts edge closer to the Esplanade, where crowds stroll back and forth, where Helsinki is full of life and gaiety, throngs and the fulfillment of the moment.

"Nobody is in Helsinki," Armi declared emphatically over her coffee in the crowded Kappeli, where crowds were walking back and forth, looking for tables and getting the waitresses all confused. Every now and then Armi waved to some acquaintance or other. Some of them stopped at our table for a minute, others she identified as "He's so-and-so." She took a leisurely bite of cake. "Nobody is in Helsinki."

"What do you mean?" The place was full. The orchestra was playing Strauss waltzes and everybody was trying to drown out the music with their chatter. "What about all these people you know?"

"They are only here because they have to be. Everybody else has left the city. What a pity my vacation just ended—"

Armi was right. Nobody is in Helsinki. Everyone who can leaves the city in the summer and turns it over to rushing Americans, hungry Germans, and crochety English old maids. Why, I do not know. Perhaps because every Finn still feels the lakes and the fields, the forests and stony coasts so clearly in his heart that he has to get away from the cities.

While we were walking to Armi's office I made up my mind. I had been a week in Helsinki, that was enough. A week of sightseeing and promenading, antique shops and bookstores, Porvoo and Runeberg, museums and movies. And every morning I had gotten up later and lazier. It was time I left Helsinki.

"I am going to Suursaari," I announced to Armi when we got to her office.

"Suursaari? Why Suursaari? When?"

"Oh, I don't know why. But everybody seems to be going, and so am I. Tomorrow afternoon."

183

FINLAND

"I will see you off."

"Fine—" I said, realizing that now I would have to go, though I was not certain that I wanted to. Suursaari, a Finnish resort. The poor work and get as far as their garden colony plots in the suburbs, the rich have their summer cottages, others visit their country relatives, and all the rest go to Suursaari, the Big Island in the Gulf of Finland. It was an island of fishermen who had once been pirates. I wanted to see them, but then I was not so certain when I heard returning vacationers speak of the quaint atmosphere and the gayness of the casino at night. Still, I had committed myself, so I was going, though pirates and fishermen, quaintness and a gay casino somehow seemed a hopeless chaos.

The South Harbor was crowded, as usual, with white ships snorting out black smoke in their eagerness to be off. On the shore there was a bustle of cabs and crowds, suitcases and innumerable packages bulging with books and fruit, the sounds of laughter, the pageant fringed with a row of flower stalls under bright awnings and umbrellas. Somehow, the Finns have the ability of making even such a sailing as this of the *Viola* on its seven-hour trip an event. More taxis—greetings and farewells, the waving of handkerchiefs, sun and beaming clouds. So much emotion that it was possible to think we were going off on a year's trip, or around the world.

There were no signs of Armi, but it was such an exciting beginning I no longer thought of backing out; I resolutely carried my baggage on board in time to hear the last imperious blowing of whistles and the last minute farewells, warnings and wishes. The gangplank was pulled down, the ship was off. The women put down their bunches of roses, the men pulled out their newspapers. The children began to shiver and feel ill. The pale lady in black disappeared into the cabin—she would emerge when we landed. The imperious blonde girl stood alone at the stern—she would stay there the whole trip, alone, with the wind blowing her hair. The young blond fellow with the Prussian haircut, turned-up nose and an amorous look began his resolute but resultless vigil between the cabin and the stern of the boat, the glance of his eyes unanswered. I settled down to enjoy the sea.

Slowly the sun disappeared. Did it shine only on Helsinki and make us glance back at the jewel-white city with longing? Ahead of us lay livid moss-green water, billowy clouds showing their dark side, a group of hopeful gulls, and loneliness. The loneliness of rocky islands, gray and stark, accented by the recurring rhythmical pattern of an occasional fertile island, richly green, backed with blue-black forest, accented by an occasional trim white yacht in the cove. The network of islands grew thinner; the islands became shreds of rock, and occasionally you could see the open water to the south, an open sea which stretched on and became one with the sky.

The southern sky grew darker. The livid green of the water became black. The islands left us, and we were sailing in a gloomy loneliness of wind and high waves. The mad cackle of the gulls became a hollow echo. The *Viola* tossed and groaned restlessly. The bow dipped into the water, surged up again, and the spray leaped up as from a fountain. Rain, cold rain. In the cabin the men had folded their newspapers and stared helplessly at their wives who felt poorly. The roses were beginning to wilt. The lady in black looked pale, but she puffed nervously at a cigarette and read a book with determination. Someone left hurriedly.

I went into the saloon, ordered coffee, and opened Heine's *Reisebilder* to read of the sunny Alps and Italy.

"Pardon, may I sit down?"

I nodded. It was the fellow with the Prussian haircut and turned-up nose. He sat down and began to talk, phrases about the weather that I could assent to and thus enter upon a conversation, a philosophical remark of how there seemed to be a storm every time he went to Suursaari—this was his fourth summer. I asked him about the island, so he told me of the various routes he had taken, of his friend who had been with him last summer and was supposed to be on the boat now but for his hangover, of the really gay night just before he had left. I agreed it must have been gay—perhaps he would like to try a cup of black coffee.

He tried. By the way, had I heard the Russians were interested in Suursaari? No? Well, a Russian battleship had been seen near there. They would not dare though, those Russians. Just let them try—he himself had spent two weeks digging ditches at the Carelian frontier. Finland decided it had to fortify—everybody was at the Carelian frontier this summer, doing his bit. And the army—long descriptions of target-shooting contests, of last year's maneuvers, and of next month's maneuvers.

Splendid, I agreed.

By the way, he had his army field-glasses with him: would I like to use them? We went out on deck, where the cold air seemed magnificent. Raw, my friend complained, but I silently disagreed. It was easier to breathe.

Land was in sight—a tiny strip of it, rising up lonely from the sea. The waves seemed determined to keep us where we were, however, and an hour later the island was still a tiny strip, with a pale light glowing invitingly from its northern tip. The ship tossed and moaned; the waiting grew unbearable. Twenty minutes more, said the captain, and immediately the women began to feel better and took their wilted roses in their arms, while the men began to fumble through the pile of suitcases and packages. Everyone stood on deck, no one minded the spray.

We rounded the northern tip of the island and headed down the eastern shore. It was nothing but a mass of gray rocky shore and dense black forest. The rain stopped, the waves ceased beating. A few minutes and we saw the breakwater. The trip was over.

The long stone breakwater curved gracefully to the shore, sheltering a cove where a score of fishing boats were in safe anchorage. Through the network of spars and rigging rose the gray storehouses and tiny wharves, the maze of red houses and mad pattern of roofs, the background of steep forested hills. To the left was a long low building near the shore, with bright light from its row of windows shining over the cove.

"That's the casino," explained my friend. "Don't you hear the music? See you there later?"

I nodded, not knowing why, perhaps only to get rid of him.

You went down the gangplank, into the crowd of men and women and children who were waiting for friends and paid no attention to you. At the shore end of the breakwater was a little building where you stood in line, got a slip of paper with a name on it, passed the slip of paper and your suitcase to one of the boys standing in another line, and were off to your island lodging.

The boy trudged on silently, and you followed, staring about at the little town. You went up a lane that was deep sand at first and slowly gave way to rougher gravel. A dozen other lanes started from anywhere and disappeared behind houses that crept up to the edge of the lane or stood casually behind a picket fence and a rough garden. Behind some of the windows you could see an oil lamp hanging above a table, throwing a weak light against the row of plants on the window sill. You kept track of the turns and corners—"two blocks" here, left turn, up, another turn, a white fence at the left, in the second gate.

The boy climbed the little porch, knocked at the door and went in. Someone got up from a creaking bed, and an old woman came out. "I did not expect anyone tonight."

Perhaps there was no room.

"Yes—only I did not expect anyone until tomorrow." She led me down the garden path, to a little toy house. "Don't bump your head," she warned as she opened the door. "Here."

I stooped very low and waited while she fumbled with a match and candle. "Here you are." I straightened myself carefully; the ceiling was just high enough for me, the room just big enough for a bed along one end, a table on one side, a wash-bowl on a stool and a small chest of drawers on the other. A small window, a couple of stools, a rag rug, and the room was so full that whenever I opened my suitcase I had to move something else out of the way to make space for it. It was fine, I decided, feeling disappointed that the window framed not the ocean but a gooseberry bush, feeling a bit hemmed in from turning too suddenly lest the wash-stand be upset or knees bump against a stool. All in all, it was fine. Now to the casino for a cup of coffee before going to bed.

The thunderstorm had cleared away, and the big island was looking its romantic best in the half light that threw nothing into glaring relief or shrouded deep shadow. The cove was calm, the lights from the anchored *Viola* crossed the water. I walked along the shore, my shoes getting more full of sand every minute, and walked up to the casino, a modern building with a glass front and a big terrace. Someone waved from a far table and came in my direction. It was the blond fellow—it was too late to turn back.

"Hello—thought you had almost forgotten to come. I have a table over here. Coffee is already ordered. . . ." We had coffee and cigarettes; we told each other about our rooms, where they were. He asked me about Germany, and I told him about America. Then he decided we would have to call each other by first names—Finns were always too formal—so he called me Toivo and I called him Arvid. We would meet on the beach in the morning. His friends would be there. We could swim, play cards, talk.

I was late the next morning. Partly because I had lost my way going back to the toy house—I lost track of the turns, they all looked alike, there were several white fences, but they were all at the right and none of them seemed to have a second gate. Partly because it took a long time to fall asleep on a straw mattress. Once I had longed for one, before I knew what they were like, but I had already had my ambition fulfilled on a walking trip in the Black Forest. You feel a bit like an adventurer at first, giving up soft modern comforts. At the same time, the straw is sharp; it pricks and tickles you every time you turn. It rustles; it keeps you awake; it lets you sleep awhile and then suddenly wakes you up again. The morning was half gone before I felt ambitious enough to get up. I sat over my breakfast for a long time—Arvid would be on the beach, anyway, surrounded by his circle of friends. I had another cigarette, read two old magazines and a week-old newspaper, and got to the beach just as Arvid was leaving for lunch. The water was invigorating, he said. I thought it was freezing and decided on a climb up to the Pirate's Column.

It was worth bruising my knee, getting my feet wet, losing the way and retracing my steps twice, for the view was superb. Far below was the village, with ships in the harbor, miles of rocky coast and forest, and the sea, appearing vast with the schooner, sails spread wide, sailing alone on its surface. To the north the coast of Finland lay blue and serene. To the south, Estonia was visible. From the east one could almost get a whiff of Russia. . . . Before me, the abrupt, neatly sliced chasm of rock with a soft carpet of moss far below.

Once, when the island was more sparsely settled, a pirate soldier had landed on Suursaari, had seen the most beautiful girl on the island and wanted to take her with him. The girl was unwilling and ran into the forest, with the man chasing wildly after her. She panted up the hill, jumped from rock to rock, stumbled, ran on. The pirate swore under his breath, came closer, grabbed, threw himself around her—and both girl and soldier plunged down into the chasm to their sudden death.

No doubt it was a prize worth striving for. Even today there is something dark and alluring about the people of the dark island, a certain majestic beauty about the old woman leading me down the garden path to the little toy house. They are proud people, these islanders. Pirates once—with the richly laden Hansa ships to plunder, caves to hide booty. Far harbors to visit, to return with a beautiful Latin bride. Then smuggling and rum-running. Their big village to return to. (There is another village three miles farther south on the island. It is like the big village, only smaller, and it has neither harbor nor church, so the people of the big village hold their heads higher.) Centuries of hard life, wresting a living from the sea, catching fish; the whole village turning out to clean the catch; a trip to Estonia to scll the fish and buy salt and flour; return with a little whisky to make the sea more cheerful—and fishing again, the smell of fish on the wharves and the lanes and in the houses in an endless cycle. . . .

In the summer the fishing boats do not move out of the harbor. There are no fish, no smells. The storehouses stand empty; the gray nets wave in the breeze. The men sit in the sun, pipe in mouth, lazily mending nets; the boys of the village stare at the city people who have come to the big island because it is different, quaint, and because there are other city people around; old women wear shawls and wrinkles and make life comfortable for the visitor in this big island village.

There are no automobiles, no trains, only two

bicycles and three women washing clothes on the shore. One cat—she ran like a scared rabbit when I came into the yard in the midnight dusk. Miscellaneous dogs. Four cows, small and dirty, mooing discontent. Two more cows and a calf, all silent. Lanes, twisting, unlabeled. One cement sidewalk, beginning suddenly and without reason, threading its way past the modernistic casino toward the blue and white cabañas on the beach where the bathers lie sprawled in the sand and sun. It was a languid existence. I could find no quarrel with it, but Arvid was tired of lying on the beach.

"Let's throw ball," he insisted.

The leather ball stung and made my hand ache each time I caught it. It grew red and tender.

"This is swell practice," Arvid enthused. "I will be in good trim for throwing hand-grenades at the maneuvers!"

Hand grenades—threatening Russians—maneuvers. Why?

"Catch! Hello, Niemi!" Turning to me again, "He is from Tampere." Then, lying down again, he would see a girl coming to the beach: "I am sure I have seen her in Tampere—now what *is* her name?"

Arvid kept me in tow. We entered upon the daily ritual of mobbing the breakwater to greet an incoming steamer, with the patronizing air of those who belonged, crushed against suitcases, dogs, blan-

kets and wilted roses, red noses and pale cheeks. If
no one from Tampere was on the boat we went back
to the casino and danced with the two girls at the
next table. Arvid would have the waitress send them
cocktails, and when the orchestra put away their
music for the night we would go with the girls, race
around the cabañas on the beach, swim in the cold
night water, sit on the benches under a tree.

"What a marvelous place, this big island," Arvid
declared. I nodded, but the following morning I
told him I had to take the next boat to Helsinki.
My friends were waiting for me in the country.
"That is too bad, you should stay longer. Maybe I
will see you in Tampere—but no, I have those maneuvers. . . ."

There were no wilted roses on the boat, only
tired people going home. I wondered what Armi
would say when I returned to Helsinki so soon.
Then I saw the girls we had danced with: they were
standing at the stern, watching the big village and
the lights dim in the distance, listening to the music
from the casino fade into the sea.

"You leaving, too?" they asked me. "We're on our
way to Helsinki. We have to be in Tampere tomorrow."

When we got to Helsinki in the morning, the
market-place was crowded. Havis Manda blinked in

FINLAND

the sun, and the waitresses were putting fresh cloths on the Kappeli tables. Men and women were streaming into the city through the arched portal of the pink granite station, and early morning tourists were rushing for the trains to Turku, Viipuri and Tampere.

VI ❦

Tampere is three hours north of Helsinki. This is short, as distances go in Finland, but it is actually shorter still because everyone stops at the halfway point to have a look at Hämeenlinna, for any one of various specific reasons: romantics, because it has a castle; hero-worshipers, because Sibelius was born here; epicureans, because it has a famous hotel. Hämeenlinna is old, older than Helsinki. For three centuries it has been a city; during all this time, however, it has steadfastly refused to grow into any sort of a city at all, and the most anyone can say of it is that it is a typical "small town." Still, the province of Häme is called Finland's heart, and Hämeenlinna is both the castle and pearl of Häme, so there you are. You cannot visit the castle because it is a women's prison. Sibelius moved out years ago, but there is a small park bearing his name and giving shelter to several trees, an ancient sacrificial stone and a monument to fallen German heroes. The hotel, after two fires, is at the height of its glory.

The castle, being a castle and a prison, stands aloof on the shore of Lake Vanajavesi. Birger Jarl started to build the castle when he surprised the stubborn pagans of Häme into submission and

Christianity in the thirteenth century; the castle was enough to keep them in submission. It is prosaic and square. It does not look exactly like a good grain elevator, but there are not windows enough to make it look like a useful factory, so it is probably satisfactory as a castle and ideal as a prison. Of course, once you know it is a prison, you can no longer call the gray granite and red brick walls mellow and soft: they suddenly become forbidding. The castle is strategically located near the southern end of a lake which winds northward and branches out into a whole network of lakes and waterfalls and rivers. Hämeenlinna should have become a city without more ado, but it restricted itself to a few hovels in the shadow of the castle. It should have been a splendid trading center with the coming of roads in the Middle Ages, for it was the meeting place of the east-west and north-south trails. Hämeenlinna still restricted itself to a few hovels. Trade was limited to furnishing wine and beer to the merchants passing through: that is probably the reason why Viipuri and Turku, Tampere and Helsinki each have their "Hämeenlinna Road."

Three hundred years ago Per Brahe took the matter in hand. His chief delight seemed to be founding cities, so he certainly had the necessary qualifications for solving Hämeenlinna's problem. He spent five days in the castle. The first two days he rested, on the third he established the city of Hämeenlinna, and on the fourth he founded a school for the new city. The fifth he no doubt spent in well-earned rest. Still the city did not grow, for the peasants seemed to prefer life anywhere but near the castle. A century after Brahe's time an impartial observer declared that "the city is in all respects like a village—except for its one straight street, which is supposed to make it look like a city."

Gustav III, to whom matters of state meant mostly staging theatricals in Drottningholm and comic opera wars against any willing victims, took a firm hand in the matter of Hämeenlinna. He solved the problem that had vexed everyone else by simply moving the city half a mile farther south, out of the castle's shadow, and bolstering its pride by declaring it the capital of Häme. There was no medieval church to focus the city around, but Gustav did the best he could under the circumstances and built a new church: outside, a round affair with a shallow dome and squat Doric columns; inside, an amphitheater with pews circling in tiers around an altar in the middle. An acre of cobblestone paving in front of the church provided a market-place, and, presto, Hämeenlinna was a city.

A fire fifty years later burned down most of the houses that had been built, but now that the burghers were in the spirit of the thing, they were not daunted in the least and proceeded to rebuild—low, Empire style houses in long, even rows. They remembered that theoretically, if they were to keep Per Brahe's reputation intact, they should have a school, so they enthusiastically built lots of schools, all kinds of schools. Later the Russians came, found the place suitable—the castle forbidding enough, the meadows ideal for parading—and built a row of barracks behind the castle. And because soldiers sometimes get sick, a Dr. Sibelius moved to Hämeenlinna. He had a son named Jean. His house is still pointed out, and everyone is quite proud of the Sibelius Park not far from the market-place. That is Hämeenlinna.

The province of Häme is a combination of woodland, extensive cultivation and old cultural monuments. To observe these qualities with fairness means staying at Hämeenlinna for a while. This is best done outside the city at the Aulanko Hotel, which began life as a manor. When the Renaissance-style château burned down, a neo-classic pavilion took its place. When that burned down, they built a hotel so modern that last summer a movie star climbed up what she thought was an observation tower—and fell into the smoke-stack. The extensive Aulanko park has woodlands (a sculptured bear in front of a deserted cave is intended to make the woodland primeval in appearance), vigorous cultivation (statues on pedestals, artificial lakes, flower beds, a "temple of love"), and old cultural relics can be surveyed at a glance by simply looking at the castle across the lake.

In Finland Proper everyone bustles with activity, chatters about business and pride in their old culture; in Carelia the people laugh gaily, and with equal ease bring tears into their eyes over a melancholy folk song; the people of Savo go briskly about clearing wildernesses. The people of Häme are tall, blond, blue-eyed—and silent. They do not waste words: when father and son went into the forest in the morning, the son remarked, "That was a rabbit," when a hare crossed their path, but it was not until when they were coming home in the evening that the father replied, "So it was."

This is hard to understand, because the Hämeans have a smiling, pastoral landscape. The forests long ago ceased to be anything but pleasant woodlands. The meadows are rich, the fields well cultivated. The lakes are small and pleasant; the hills, low and rolling. The people, hard-working, persevering—and silent. The rest of Finland came into contact with Swedish culture, or Slavic temperaments, or the armies of Europe anywhere from the Neva and the Danube to their own back yard. The Hämeans came into contact with a simpler but stronger force: the land itself. That is Häme.

FINLAND

This is the part of the land where the Finns first stopped when they came to Finland. It is here that they took stones like the one in Sibelius Park (smaller, not much different from the Plymouth Rock) and studded them with coins and needles while sages danced around, enticing good luck with well-chosen words. It is here that the Finns most resisted Christianity, but the resistance was systematically crushed: if there was a sacred grove near by, then the church was built there; since the pagans considered the cock a sacred animal, the cock was put on the weather-vanes of the Christian churches, to coax the pagans to worship. A castle was built to make sure they would remain Christians and stop raiding Turku. They stopped, and for centuries they have lived a quiet uneventful life close to the land. They are silent, for what is there to talk about?

Alexis Kivi has movingly portrayed this life of Häme in his *Seven Brothers*. When the *Kalevala* appeared a century ago to give birth to Finnish literature, Kivi made it of age a quarter century later. Like Lönnrot, Kivi was born in southern Finland, the son of a poor village tailor; like Lönnrot, he suffered great privation to get an education; but Lönnrot died an honored old man, while Kivi's death at the age of thirty-eight scarcely meant anything to the Finnish public. "He lived only from autumn to Christmas," the darkest days of the year, and he never saw brightness or gaiety come into his life. His sacrifices ruined his health; his writings did not bring money enough to pay his debts. For ten years he lived alone in the country, in the backyard cottage of a maiden lady who sheltered him from the world and gave him food so he could live. It was a tiny cottage—there is a reproduction of it in the Seurasaari outdoor museum near Helsinki—a little entry and a room just big enough for a stove in one corner, a bed, a table under the window. Here he wrote his *Lea*, the play which founded the Finnish Theater; it was the only success to come to him in his lifetime. Here he wrote his poems, another play, the *Heath Cobblers*, and his novel, the *Seven Brothers*. He worked in feverish haste, suffering under the double load of debt and increasing ill health. His loneliness, his restlessness sometimes drove him to Helsinki to seek forgetfulness and solace. A worse sickness brought what the doctors of the time called "melancholia." It brought death, and to the world, a novel with realism and humor and seven young heroes.

The seven brothers of Jukola inherited a farm which had gone downhill, because their father had preferred hunting bears to farming—until a bear killed him—and because their mother had worried herself to death. The seven brothers preferred hunting and adventure, too, and when the sexton made them learn to read and write, and locked them in a room when they would not, they fled through the window and into the forest, deserting their home, the neighbors they could not get along with, and "civilization." In the forest they could live by hunting; they could fight, play, live like healthy young animals. The Häme forest they fled into was beautiful, mysterious and full of legend, but the Jukola brothers had to struggle against winter, starvation and the dangers lurking in the forest. Slowly, with Hämean slowness, they lost their prejudices and their stubbornness. After ten years in the forest they returned to their home, tired of adventure and eager to learn to read and write, to live with their neighbors in peace, to marry, to plow the fields of Jukola until they should be as rich as any of the fields of Häme.

The fields of Häme give way to Tampere, Finland's biggest industrial city. To call Tampere big is misleading, for its population is only sixty thousand; to call it industrial is deceiving, because it looks more like a garden city. It is still more deceiving to hear the natives boastingly call their city Finland's Manchester, for it does not bear the slightest resemblance to Manchester, England or Manchester, New Hampshire. This comparison can probably be credited to James Finlayson, who was

Tampere's first industrial giant. Finlayson can be pardoned for seriously boasting that Tampere was as fine as Manchester, because he himself came from Glasgow. Anyone can boast seriously about Tampere, for it is as model as any industrial city can be.

Tampere is built on a mile-wide isthmus between two lakes: Näsijärvi on the north hurls its waters through the Tammerkoski rapids, with a drop of fifty-eight feet, into Pyhäjärvi on the south. This isthmus was occupied as far back as the Stone Age, and it is not far from here that the Pirkkala men went north to exploit the Lapps in the Middle Ages. In the sixteenth century Tampere was a prosperous village, with numerous mills grinding the grain from the Häme fields into flour, but in the seventeenth century it was nothing more than an estate with a sawmill on the Tammerkoski. Per Brahe looked the place over, to see whether a city there "would be a help or a detriment to the land." Perhaps he decided he had done enough in declaring Hämeenlinna a city, for Tampere was allowed to continue being an estate with a sawmill.

Tampere began to spin flax in 1759, and a few years later Gustav III, who finished Brahe's work in Hämeenlinna, came to Tampere and decided that a city there would not be detrimental to the land. He established a city, and along with it, set up a

205

brewery. It was not an especially noble beginning for a city, but when the brewery was closed down a few years later the citizens of Tampere threatened to move out if it were not promptly reopened.

In 1819 Alexander I confirmed Gustav's view: he was enthusiastic about the possibilities of Tampere as an industrial center, and the next year he sent James Finlayson, formerly of Glasgow, more recently of Moscow, to see what he could do in Tampere. Finlayson was enthusiastic, and soon he was overflowing with joy, because Alexander gave him plenty of land on the Tammerkoski as a present, a big loan without interest, and complete customs freedom. His cotton factory flourished. Other factories came, and now over two hundred industrial enterprises crowd Tampere, turning out textiles and machinery, shoes and paper, airplanes and rubber boots. It is Finland's largest industrial city, it is Finland's Manchester.

There is no need to avoid this city. On the contrary, I wish some American city planners, housing experts and industrialists would take a look at Tampere. The factories rise from parks, with flowerbeds and trees and statues making the smoke-stacks an inconspicuous detail. The streets are broad, tree-lined boulevards. There are promenades, more statues, museums—one of them remodeled from a granary designed by Engel. There are buildings whiter and more modern than those in Helsinki. Old buildings are quickly replaced by shining new ones, and every year sees whole new quarters of tall apartment houses to shelter Tampere's workers. The city has two legitimate theaters, the Tampere stage and the workers' stage. There are restaurants overlooking factories, and restaurants overlooking lakes.

An old wooden church stands on the edge of the market-place, with a dome and a spire like a dunce cap, while another church lies hidden behind a very secular fountain. Nobody seems to care that the Russian church is falling rapidly to ruin near the railroad tracks. In a park opposite a factory rises a hotel that looks like a church. Finally, there is a new gray granite church with murals of nude men and women and children filling all the walls, looking as if they thought the most natural thing to do before the Ascension was to scrub their bodies glowing pink and clean in the *sauna*.

There are views in Tampere: to the north, the broad Näsijärvi, the Poet's Way; to the south, Pyhäjärvi, becoming the Kokemäki river and flowing to the Gulf of Bothnia. There are views from hill-top parks, over the smoke-stacks that pour out no smoke, over the spreading suburbs, over lake and forest and rolling Häme hills.

If Savonlinna immediately suggests a trip to Punkaharju, then Tampere has the Vehoniemenharju,

which is even more beautiful. Being Hämeans, the
people do not talk much about it, but I doubt if
there is a much finer spot in all Finland. The bus
heads east from Tampere, past the gray medieval
church of Messukylä (at one time Tampere used to
belong to the Messukylä parish; now Messukylä is
about to be swallowed by Tampere) to Kangasala,
with another gray medieval church. This church has
a portrait of Queen Karin inside, a "bleeding stone"
outside. You see, a girl pleading her innocence was
executed on this stone—and she was innocent, else
the stone would not still be bleeding for the poor
maiden's heart. Of course I did not see even a red
stain, but that is the legend, and I would not quarrel with it.

Two cups of coffee in Kangasala fortified me for
the ten-kilometer walk to Vehoniemenharju. I began
with great expectations, and my enthusiasm grew
with every kilometer. As soon as the road left the
village it led up a ridge, with a pond on the right
and a lake on the left. Tall pine trees framed the
meadows sloping down to the lake gleaming in the
sun. Then the road went down into the meadow and
plunged into a cool glade, with a gaily painted
gypsy cart under the trees, a horse tethered to a tree,
and a gypsy girl running wild and staring at me as
I passed. Surely a hand moved the curtain in the
tiny window of the cart? The glade grew darker, and

I went faster. Had the woodland become primeval forest, a Gothic wilderness? Full of bloodthirsty gypsies and hissing serpents? I told myself a gruesome story, like the macabre stories the seven brothers of Jukola used to tell when they were around the camp fire and there were mysterious noises, a gleam of light, the cracking of a twig. The story of the ancient white serpent with the marvelous crown on his head. He had been king of the serpents for centuries. People saw him but seldom, and then he always glided along the ground with the swiftness of lightning. Once a knight did see it resting on a rocky mound, its crown gleaming in the bright sun. The knight hesitated only for a moment, then rode boldly up the mound, seized the rich crown from the serpent's head with the tip of his sword, spurred on his horse and rode away with the swiftness of the wind and the clouds.

Immediately the angry serpents sprang up from all sides and began to pursue the bold thief. They hissed and slid over the ground, and, curled into rings, they rolled along after the knight like a thousand colored hoops on a hillside, hissing angrily, going faster and faster, until it was not long before they caught up to the knight. The snakes twined themselves tightly around the stallion's legs. They climbed upward, and the man's danger became greater than ever.

FINLAND

The knight threw down his feathered cap to the snakes, hoping to stay them. The serpents stopped. The cap was seized and immediately torn into shreds. Another moment, and even the shreds were gone. The serpents started after the thief again, and a cloud of dust rose up along the winding road.

The knight urged on his stallion, faster and faster. Blood flowed from the wounds where the snakes had bitten the horse, and foam rushed out of his mouth. Into the forest fled the knight, but even the brush did not keep the serpents from following close behind. The rider came to a river, and with a shout of joy he rode into the water. The snakes were at the river's edge; they splashed into the swift-flowing stream. They swam across with the speed of the storm, and the water rose up behind them in an angry white foam.

The knight rode ever onward. Ever closer and closer the band of serpents crept upon him.

In the distance he saw a ring of fire circling a hillside, burning all the grass and the brush and the trees. He wrapped himself in his wet cloak, spurred on the horse, and disappeared in the flames. But not for a moment did the serpents hesitate: straightway they, too, went into the fire.

Like Apollo riding through the clouds the knight plunged into the flames. Once more he pressed the spurs, and once more the stallion strove onward, and then fell, forgetting spurs and wounds and blood and flames forever. The knight stood on the mountain-top, saved from fire and the thousand enemies, the thousand serpents which had perished in the flames. The hero stood on the hill-top, looking over the soaring forest.

I did not try to decide whether the story was eastern Finnish, full of Slavic color and embroidery, or western and matter-of-fact. It was probably true to the Finnish spirit, showing what this vast Finnish forest might have held for the Finnish imagination, which peopled the forest with horseless riders, white stallions, witches and ghosts. It might have been nothing more than Kivi's "melancholia," and I had long ago passed the gypsies, who were only harmless knife grinders or horse thieves. The road was climbing another ridge, which meant another lake and the sun blazing through the tall pines. It was a stately ridge, with a lake on each side, called the "Emperor's Ridge" because Alexander I visited it on his trip to Tampere. Down. Now the lakes came so close to each other there was nothing but a narrow strip of road between them. Up.

Another climb and it was Vehoniemenharju at last, with a hotel that is nothing more than a red country house, and a tower that is nothing more than a wobbling platform precariously set on the highest spot, overlooking a lake on the left and a lake on the right. The chain of ridges stretches to Kangasala like a huge green necklace along fringed blue lakes. The sky looks immense. The trees sigh softly, and far below the waves are lapping against the rocks. Far in the distance you can see the lonely meadows of Liuksiala, where Queen Karin lived with her tragic memories and listened to the wind sighing through the pines and the waves lapping against the lonely shore. The Finnish countryside lies there with its lakes and meadows and forests, a nature that is beautiful but harsh, a landscape that is serene but mysteriously sad.

The bus back to Tampere speeds up and down the ridges, pauses at Kangasala, passes the Russian church falling to ruin, and turns into Häme Street and the Häme bridge over the rapids. This bridge is short, as bridges go, but it is also a sculptor's masterpiece. Against a background of landscaped embankments, factories and smoke-stacks, are four statues: the hunter and merchant, the tax collector and the maid of Finland, all tall and broad-shouldered, naked and serene. In Finland there are no statues of generals. Statues of poets are much more numerous, and most of them are more imaginative than the stolid Runeberg on the Esplanade. War memorials generally show a naked soldier with an upraised sword instead of angels with palms. Statues of Finns at work abound—naked Finns with an anvil, Finns with a hammer or a pelt slung over a shoulder—symbolic of their pioneers molding a nation out of the northern wilderness. Now the Finns want to raise a monument to *sisu*.

Sisu is the dominant Finnish character trait. It has been translated as "guts," but actually the word is not translatable, for it is a many-sided, positive and negative, good and bad feature of the Finn. Sooner or later, everything the Finn does or does not do is labeled *sisu,* for in the last analysis, it is not only a fundamental Finnish character trait, it is the Finnish character.

Finland is beautiful, but it is harsh and poor. The story of Finland is the story of the storm and stress of a people who have had a hard fate, who have suffered need, who have had to renounce ease and comfort and peace. The Finns have met the challenge with *sisu,* with toughness and strength and tenacity. With infinite pains they have cleared the wilderness, and the struggle has left its imprint on their character.

Someone has suggested that if a Russian, a Swede and a Finn were placed in a stony field and told to go to work, the Russian would sing and pretend to work half the day; the Swede would mutter and work until the afternoon; the Finn would look stolidly at the field and work hard until dusk. And the

FINLAND

Russian would have accomplished nothing, the Swede would have cleared away the smaller rocks, while the Finn would have spent his day carrying away all the big stones from the field.

This is true of all walks of Finnish life. In England you see elderly gentlemen fishing patiently on the Thames, in the rain, intent on their task of doing nothing. In Paris you see these same men sitting all day long on the quays of the Seine, with a curious man or two and a few boys looking on. In Finland the elderly schoolteacher digs trenches on the frontier, and the philosopher turns to plowing a field or building a stone wall.

The Finn works hard when he has a wilderness before him to clear. He is a pioneer: Finland has been built because the people have had much land and freedom. As soon as civilization has come, bringing convention and political oppression, the Finn has retreated farther away, into the vastness of the miles of primeval forest and chains of lonely lakes. Here, alone, free to do as he pleased, he cleared the forest and carried away the rocks and was pleased. He worked hard, and as soon as the task was done he sat down and was bewildered.

Per Brahe was amazed at this Finnish temperament. He complained that the Finns would not work to produce more than they could consume. That was laziness, he asserted, and with laziness came drunkenness. This latter deplorable fault he blamed on tobacco: when the Finnish soldiers returned from the Thirty Years' War in Germany they brought tobacco with them, and every man, woman and child immediately succumbed to the habit. (It should be stopped, Brahe suggested, and tobacco sold only in the pharmacies for the use of the sick.) At the same time Brahe noted that "whenever these Finns come to Sweden or elsewhere, each one of them works as hard as three men, and they are fast in their work."

Brahe did not stop to consider that perhaps the Finns produced only enough for themselves because the excess would have gone into Swedish coffers. He did not stop to think that the Finnish winter can be gloomy, cold and enervating, with the sun in captivity and all nature brooding, and that a drink might not be out of place. He did not stop to consider that the hardiness and prowess of the Finnish soldiers, who were so useful in Sweden's armies, was a result of the centuries-long struggle against nature, a struggle which called for the utmost that a man could give. It is this same spirit which drives the Finnish athletes to victory.

The Finn is an individualist, else he would not have sought the solitude of the forest and the hardships of the forest. The Finnish town is not like a European town where the farmers live huddled together, surrounded by walls and the shadow of a castle, where the men and women go out to their strips of field in the morning. The Finnish town is simply a church and a school and a store, while the Finnish farm is out in the country, surrounded by lakes and forests. The forest, in turn, has had its effect on the Finnish character. It has made the Finn gloomy, it has made him a mystic. The Finn worships his forest and stands in awe before it—surely this was the land for a shamanistic religion to flourish. It has made him a poet, for if the forest is gloomy, it is beautiful, too. The *Kalevala* reflects this mystic Finnish forest: it is the poetry of the forest. The forest has made the Finn fatalistic: there are the immutable forces of nature, one can do no more than accept. Perhaps that is why the Finnish newspapers carry the obituaries on the front page and begin the news meekly on page three. The forest has made him suspicious of change, for surely everything will always be the same—nothing changes: to this day in parts of eastern Carelia food is placed on the graves in the cemeteries. It has always been done. The spirit lives, the spirit will need food. First, last and always, the forest has called for *sisu*.

These elements of Finnish character—the obstinate individualism and tenacity coupled with the forest-engendered mysticism—are reflected in the *Kalevala*. Ilmarinen shows the enterprising tenacity of the Finnish worker: his Sampo was not forged until four previous attempts had been in vain; he does not win the maid of Pohjola before he has unflinchingly performed three perilous tasks. Wäinämöinen is his poetic counterpart, delighting in the mystery, the poetry and the magic of the forest. Kullervo lives the morose, depressed existence the forest can also bring forth: brooding and sullen and full of gloom. There is something of that brooding, gloomy quality in every Finn: he can rarely be completely carefree and gay. He feels more at home listening to a Finnish folksong—and Finnish folksongs are among the world's saddest.

This *sisu* of living an individualistic life in the forest has also produced faults in the Finnish character. It has brought, curiously enough, jealousy and suspicion, traits that are reflected throughout all Finnish life. This suspicion is balanced with trust: in old Finnish houses doors were never locked, for there was no reason to suspect that anyone might come in but as a guest. Nevertheless, individualism breeds suspicion of what the other fellow might be up to, jealousy if he seems to be getting ahead where another one does not. These faults are fundamentals of *sisu,* for lacking trust in anything but his own endeavors, the Finn does things himself, resents outside forces, suspects that others are working toward opposite or conflicting goals. *Sisu* seems like a kind of obstinacy, directed against nature (and sometimes against fellow man), an obstinacy which even becomes a *pirullisuus,* a damnedness: when a Finn starts something he will be damned if he does not carry it through to the end, come what may.

This individualistic effort of the Finn applying his *sisu* to the forest has demanded just as much strength and perseverance of the Finnish woman. She has worked just as long and just as hard as her husband—not only in the home, giving birth to children, cooking and cleaning, making clothes, doing a hundred odd tasks, but also in the fields, planting and hoeing, making hay, bringing in the harvest, milking cows. Thus the women, doing more than a fair share of the work, have won esteem and a position of independence for themselves.

Three such women appeared a thousand years ago in the *Kalevala.* Joukahainen declared that "Good the counsel of my father, and my mother's counsel better." Another hero, Lemminkäinen, did not follow his mother's advice, so he met death. Here the *sisu* of that noble woman really began, for she went to superhuman efforts to bring her son back to life after his mutilated body had been thrown into the river of the dead. The third heroic woman is Louhi, the mistress of Pohjola and the prototype of all Finnish women. She does not want gold or silver, for they are trivialities. She is not thinking of herself, but of the welfare of the race, when she desires a magic Sampo which shall bring food and warmth to the dismal Northland. When her daughter is married to Ilmarinen, Louhi gives her advice on a woman's duty:

> Thou wilt always need in future
> Ready wit and clear perception,
> And thy thoughts must all be prudent,
> Firmly fixed thy understanding,
> Eyes of keenness in the evening,
> Ears of sharpness in the morning.

Today this Kalevalic Finnish woman has a position of equality with men, and men have not bitterly opposed the granting of legal status and rights to women. The first advances were made during the reign of Alexander II: the law of 1863 declared women of age at twenty-five years and gave them the right to vote in local elections. In 1906, without any long suffrage campaign, women were given the franchise on terms of equality with men—Finnish women were thus the first in Europe to have these rights—and in the following year they had nineteen women sitting in parliament! A new law in 1926 opened all professions, except the right to preach from a pulpit or become an army officer, to the women. That is certainly equality. You find women as architects, dentists and lawyers. You find women running street-cars and driving taxicabs; you see them carrying heavy hods of cement at building constructions. They fill the post offices and banks. They shirk no kind of work: homes and factories and fields are their domains. If any of them have time left to spare, they spend that in voluntary social work. In the Lotta Svärd, feeding their husbands or brothers or lovers in the National Guard. Women scrub you in the *saunas,* and it is a rare barber shop where you can find a man to give you a hair cut.

That is one side of the picture. In the United States energetic women go into business, the others marry. In Finland, energetic women marry and the rest remain old maids. With marriage, however, the Finnish woman does not give up her career; she simply adds home-making to the list of her activities. A cousin of mine is an architect; when she married, she chose an architect for a husband, and now they work together. When another cousin married a chemical engineer in a small-town factory, she moved her dentist's office to the small town and went on merrily with her career. And Aunt Mimi, who is a farmer's wife, goes on teaching school. She is proud of her career, but she is prouder still when she is addressed as *emäntä,* which does not mean lady or Mrs. but implies much more, that she is a home-maker. She is very proud of that title *emäntä.*

I have said that the Finn is an independent creature, self-reliant, suspicious, cautious in trusting others. That is true. At the same time the Finn is highly co-operative. He understands the difficulties of others, and he is willing to help the other out of those difficulties. He understands that by a common front, by co-operation, he is able to get more out of life for others and for himself. Seven thousand co-operatives now cover the country from end to end: consumers', distributors' and manufacturers' co-operatives, dairy co-operatives, housing and banking and insurance co-operatives. There is not a community that does not have its co-operative store, an independent local enterprise, with connections in the big co-operative headquarters in Helsinki. The factories and stores look as modern as tomorrow. Indeed, the co-operative movement is only forty years old, but more than one third of the population is enrolled in some co-operative enterprise.

Many Finnish homes have a reproduction of a certain painting on their walls: two men in fur caps are talking on a wintry night before a red cottage dimly seen in the background. It is a historic moment, just after the news of the "February Manifesto" spread through the land: Hannes Gebhard is telling his friend Serlachius that "We must do something to make our people strong enough to withstand the Russian oppression." With that statement the Pellervo Society was born, a society to educate the people of Finland, especially the farmers, to co-operative action. The government made co-operatives legal, and, under the guidance of the Pellervo Society, producers' co-operatives, with banks to supply them with capital, sprang up. Consumers' organizations followed, and within six years a central buying agent for the co-operatives, Hankkija, was established. In 1914 the SOK was established to produce goods for the co-operatives, and it has grown to embrace scores of factories in Helsinki and Viipuri, Oulu and Vaajakoski. They produce everything from bags to bicycles, candy to clothes, furniture, shoe polish to mouth wash, nails and matches, building tiles and ink, with everything in between.

With all this complexity, however, the farmers, whose welfare was to be improved, have not been forgotten. There have been agricultural societies in Finland for over a century, and their organization has grown into a complex union of local and central societies, agricultural banks, and even a political organization handling the legal aspects of agriculture with power that is sometimes almost bureaucratic. The co-operatives, likewise, work effectively with the agricultural organizations and give strong financial support to agriculture.

If agricultural conditions were to be improved,

there had to be an improvement in the home itself. The same year of deep oppression that gave birth to the Pellervo Society also brought to life the women's Martha Society. This society made its task the improvement of conditions in the home: better home economics, scientific child care, a new garden under the kitchen window, the importance of fresh air, textiles to brighten up a drab room. I remember a ride with one of the Martha executives through a part of rural Finland. She explained to me how they chose poor families of their community, gave them paint, young fruit trees and shrubs, a few suggestions, and then told them to go ahead. We were on our way to visit one of these families; we drove up a country lane and stopped before a simple but charming small cottage set in an attractive garden. The Martha executive panted out of the car, waved her hand and said, "Now we come to a humble cottage . . ."

I gave up trying to be sociological, but the next day I was taken to Vaajakoski, to the SOK factories. I would have preferred going five miles farther on, to Jyväskylä, which I have never seen, but I had to content myself with Vaajakoski. I did not keep count of the number of factory buildings, but I remember that I did come away with a collection of nails, matches, and a big box of chocolates. They also manufacture brushes, paper bags, margarine, wire and furniture, in a group of modern factories surrounding a beautiful lake. The factories are all white, of course, just as most Finnish factories are. (There is a mountain facing the town: the government had plans ready to scoop out a cave in the rock for a munitions plant.) The workers' homes are modern cottages on the edge of the forest. The workers also have a modern co-operative store, their own beach, their athletic club, a restaurant finer than Schrafft's, and frequent bus service to Jyväskylä. It is so attractive, all in all, that the youth is quite willing to desert the farm to work in a factory—the young men chopping off wire into little bits, the young girls packing assorted sizes of nails into boxes for eight hours a day. How could one be contented with staying on a farm?

Older than the Pellervo Society, to uplift the farmers, or the Martha Society, to raise woman's position in the home, is the sixty-year-old youth movement (*Nuorisoseurajärjestö*) which grew out of Snellman's nationalistic principles. The task here has been to establish local societies for the improvement of youth, to make them, first of all, conscious of their nationality, and then content to stay at home, on the farm. In Mikkeli there is a school where training is given for leadership in this work; it is an old estate, with the old mansion turned into a dormitory and the stone barn transformed into classrooms. The organization now has over sixty thousand members, and in one year alone they have put on more than five thousand plays, ten thousand meetings and twelve thousand speeches. They have their popular education groups, their speech choruses, their glee clubs. They collect folklore; they preserve local arts and crafts. They learn to love Finland, their own part of Finland, their village, home, and the rowans and birches growing in the yard.

It is a hard life, and the Finn, too, dreams of a day when life might be easier. When he is old he would like to rest, living in a little cottage in the backyard of the farm, or even in a corner of the big kitchen, while the younger ones, the married son or daughter, carry on the work. It is hard work; the soil does not yield much. Youth becomes restless— from childhood on, life has meant to them hard work, loneliness, the prospect of more hard work, responsibility, worries, being ever satisfied with little, and finally a feeble, tired old age in a corner of the kitchen while their children go through the same cycle. Is there no hope?

I remember an old peasant grandmother in the Odenwald, paring potatoes near the kitchen stove. So, I was from America? Then I might know her son; he is in America, too, in some city called New York. She was surprised I did not know her son. "He is big and strong—he will get rich in America," she assured me.

I told her I was sure of it.

In Finland, too, there are mothers and fathers whose children have gone to America, where one has a chance to live and breathe, a chance to grow rich, perhaps. Poor families save and scrape for years, putting pennies aside, until there is enough to send one of the family to America. He works hard and saves, sends money home so that another brother or sister can come. Another, until all are in America. Only the old father and mother are left at home; they cannot bear to part with their lake and forest and the meadow behind the *sauna*. Letters come, of course, but through the years they get more infrequent—there is not much time to write letters in America; there is not much to write about—finally perhaps a letter at Christmas, then a lonely death on the lonely farm.

And their sons in far-off America? They work hard. It is no easy life drawing wire, or pushing a wheelbarrow, or digging in a mine. The city seems cramped and ugly. The air is heavy; there is no space to breathe. If one had a little farm, how splendid life would be! It is not hard to get: the Finn has *sisu;* he can save, he can get along with little. Soon he has his farm and is proud. It is just like at home, in Finland. The hills are there, the lake is not far.

226

Pines and birches fill the forest, and stones cover the fields. He is happy.

The next summer life is complete, for there is a *sauna* in the yard. A *sauna* is a fine thing.

Thank God the town is behind those hills. It will be an easy matter to clear the stones from the fields, then the hay will be good.

Listen—the wind sighs just as it used to in Finland. What more could a man want?

Gallen-Kallela once painted a picture which raised a furor in Finnish art circles. It need not have, for it is typically Finnish: sad, full of gloom and foreboding. The artist called it *Problem* at first; later he changed the title to *Symposium*. Four men, holloweyed, somberly dressed, are grouped around a table with wine bottles and half-empty glasses, wreathed in smoke. One of the men is asleep, his head covered with his arm. The other three, Kajanus and Sibelius and the artist himself, are looking calmly at a part of a dark wing, death-like and mysterious before them, their problem. The men are silent, deep in thought, lost in the infinite sadness of life.

If the picture were Russian you could hear an intellectual declare that "Existence is tedious. It is a senseless, dirty business, this life, and goes heavily."

A Russian, yes.

The Finn? He sees the infinite sadness of life, the

gloom of the forest, the hardships of existence. Then he sweeps away the wineglasses, lets fresh air into the room, bids farewell to mystic introspection and goes briskly about his work. Self-reliant, strong, determined that he will either get the best of life—or death. That is *sisu*.

VII ✒

THE RED COTTAGE

EVERYBODY IN Finland knows that "Rauma is always Rauma," because the good burghers of that city have stated it so often and so emphatically that it has become a proverb. It is not self-defense, or boasting; the Rauma burghers are too proud to state it as anything but a fact.

Another fact, not mentioned by the Rauma burghers, is that it takes four hours to reach their city from Tampere. The Helsinki-Tampere train is an express, so rapid that soot dances on the plates in the dining-car and descends, paprika fashion, on the food. The train along the Kokemäki river valley toward Rauma is an ordinary one: it crawls along, and the soot covers your face and hands. The last straw comes at Peipohja: here the train goes off to the right, to Pori. The Rauma burghers wanted it to come to them, but when the state built it to Pori, instead, because the Kokemäki happens to flow to Pori, Rauma went stanchly ahead and built its own railroad. So in Peipohja you change to a sort of laughable toy train (locomotive Swiss, vintage 1898) that bumps and sways and rattles and stops every five minutes and eventually gets to Rauma.

It has been my fate to shuttle back and forth on

this track time and again, for to me Tampere is the parting of the ways. A pleasant city, Tampere, but I have a bevy of aunts waiting for me in Rauma, and another bevy in Virrat. A day's boat trip north on Näsijärvi lies Virrat, my mother's home. A four-hour train trip west ends at Rauma, where my father was born. All in all, it is not a bad train ride. We follow Näsijärvi for a while—just so that I can see the sparkling water and the tempting prospect of a boat trip to Virrat when it is too late and I am on the stuffy train. Then we get into the Kokemäki river valley. This river was born of Näsijärvi, and its valley is important. Here the Finns heard St. Henry, here Lalli killed him. There is a rest home on the right, and a hospital for the insane on the left, if things go from bad to worse. That is Nokia, with the overflow of Tampere's factories, and here is what is left of Pirkkala, the medieval business center. Here the astute Pirkkala men hit upon the scheme of first monopolizing trade with the Lapps and then taxing them, with the king's permission, because as soon as the Lapps were taxed they could be called citizens.

One Pirkkala leader was Matti. (A man is not Tom, Dick or Harry in Finland—he is Matti.) Nothing is known of his business ability, but he was celebrated far and wide as a brave hero. The Russians had an exceptional hero, too, named Pohto, an exceedingly strong man. They sent Pohto to Finland, suggesting that the Swedes' best man should meet him in a duel. No one dared to accept the challenge, so word was finally sent to Matti. Matti was ready; he demanded only that the fight should not take place until the following morning. Matti knew that Pohto (like Achilles) had been charmed so he was not vulnerable; Matti spent the night lessening these charms with even stronger incantations.

Next day the two heroes rowed in their skiffs across the lake to the island which had been chosen for the combat. Matti pushed Pohto's skiff with one determined heave straight back to the mainland shore. "The one who stays here to rest will not need a boat," he sneered to the astonished Russian.

Pohto answered by seizing his sword: he slashed Matti's right hand so hard that it was severed. Matti fell on his knees in pain. "Why, you jump like a *kurki!*" laughed Pohto.

Matti was not in the least perturbed. He was left-handed, he had lost only his useless right hand. He jumped up with a shout: "I still know how to fly!" Then he sliced off Pohto's head. As a reward Matti received Lauko manor on the Vesilahti and took the name Kurki, which means heron. From him the famous Kurki family is descended. That was in the fourteenth century. By the fifteenth century the Kurki family was quite respectable; it was producing bishops and abbesses, governors and judges, and just plain warriors. It also produced Klaus Kurki, who burned his wife Elina to death, thereby giving her greater immortality than came to the share of most medieval women. Elina has gone down in history as the heroine of one of the finest medieval Finnish ballads.

Elina Stenbock saw Klaus Kurki, a dashing young hero, ride into her mother's courtyard with a hundred men with golden swords, a hundred horses with silver bridles. Klaus asked for Elina's hand, and after the proper hesitation, she accepted.

Perhaps Klaus was too dashing a young hero: he had had a wife before, and now he had a housekeeper, young Kirsti, who was in love with him and jealous of the new mistress in Lauko manor. Kirsti told Klaus that his wife was unfaithful. "Prove it," demanded Klaus, "and I will burn Elina to death and give you five dresses and the keys to the manor."

The scheming Kirsti suggested that Klaus tell his wife that he had to go on a business trip, far away, to the Northland.

Elina sighed, patted her young son on the head and pleaded with Klaus that he should "go half-way and speak half words, drink only half a glass and hurry back, for I have but a few short weeks to live."

As soon as he was gone, Kirsti began to work. She had made a silken bed in the finest room of the manor; she enticed Elina into the room and called in the manservant Uolevi—and locked them together in the room. Then she hurried back of the hill to get Klaus.

What could be more conclusive evidence? Klaus set fire to the house.

Elina put her hand out of the window. "Do not lose my ring, if you must lose the bearer," she pleaded. Klaus cut off the finger with his sword. Elina held her son from the window. "Do not kill your son, if you must burn her who gave him birth." Klaus swore: the son was not his. So went the young mistress Elina, who was "lovely of face, lovely in all ways."

Scarcely a month later all but one of the horses in the Lauko stables grew sick and died. Klaus sat on the roadside and wept.

Christ walked by, dressed as an old man. "Why weep, Klaus?"

"I have burned my wife, my son."

Christ nodded. "I know. I know her. She is sitting at God's feet, a golden book in her hand, a little boy in her lap. I also know Klaus Kurki."

"And—where is he?"

"In hell."

Klaus rode away on his horse, over marshes, over the ridge, to the shore of the lake. He rode into the water and disappeared under the waves.

FINLAND

However, this is a train trip to Rauma. Because it takes all of four hours, there are two long stops where the passengers pour into the station restaurant for coffee. Then there is Peipohja, with the Rauma train waiting. There is the last impatient half hour down a straight valley with forests and no view, then a meadow or two, a water tower on a granite knoll, another meadow, a medieval stone church, a row of Rauma backyards, finally the station, with two aunts and three cousins standing on the platform wondering if I am really coming.

Rauma is always Rauma. That is to say, life goes on there as it has always gone on. When Rauma laid out a new street five hundred years ago, they named it King Street. There is no king in Finland today, but why should the name be changed? If, say, the family Anundila built a house in Rauma two centuries ago, it is still called Anundila, even though the family Poselli might have owned it for a hundred and ninety years. When the church of the Trinity, built circa 1300, burned down three hundred years ago, the Rauma burghers did not build a new church; they simply walked a few blocks west on Sundays to the church of the Holy Cross, built circa 1400. When the town burned down, the burghers rebuilt it again, and the town crier would call, "Twelve o'clock and all is well—may God always keep the city from fire and flames—twelve o'clock and all is well!"

No one knows how old Rauma is. It is known, though, that exactly fifty years before Columbus came to America the king of Sweden sent a letter to the city of Rauma and told the burghers they could enjoy the same rights as the burghers of Turku. At that time the city had a Franciscan monastery at the northern end of the city, a rich monastery which owned fields even in Ostrobothnia. Not far away, in the center of the city, was the town church and the market-place. Both have since disappeared, leaving only a few gray stones, too big to carry away, and a controversy over the original name of the market-place: was it the Fish Square? or was it the Cow Pasture? At any rate, they were simple days, and the Rauma burghers used to say "Peace on earth—and a priest in every parish."

The peace gave way to two fires and a plague. On top of that, Gustav Vasa ordered the monastery disbanded, just after the monks had gotten very gay murals for the church from Bishop Kurki, the son of that Klaus Kurki who had burned his wife. The church made an excellent granary, and for a time Gustav Vasa let it go at that.

Not for long, though. Gustav was not through with Rauma yet, but he meant to be. He did not see why Rauma should exist at all. It was much more logical to have a city on the Gulf of Finland, so he founded Helsinki. He published the decree, but no one seemed anxious to move to a city which existed merely on paper. Then Gustav ordered everyone in Rauma to move to Helsinki, promising them many advantages. It was a sorry fate to meet just after they had given Gustav plenty of gold to retain Rauma as their "eternal property," just after they had named King Street for him in gratitude. They refused to move to Helsinki.

Gustav threatened the Rauma burghers with death. They bribed the officials. Gustav fined them; they paid the fines cheerfully—and remained where they were. After five years the burghers began packing their goods and possessions and reluctantly moved to Helsinki, but Helsinki did not flourish even with the good example set by the people of Rauma. Gustav told them to return to Rauma.

Back home again, the people of Rauma sighed with relief, but too soon: a few years later they faced an even worse fate, a more ignominious end: the next king, Johan, decided that the Rauma burghers should move to Pori, that rival city to the north of them. The fate was averted at the last moment: Johan was not as adamant as his father had been; he was easier to bribe.

Bad fortune followed Rauma. There was another plague. The roof of the church collapsed. Then, three hundred years ago, while the Rauma burghers were out celebrating May Day, a third of the city burned down, and the church lay in ashes. The grain was swept out of the monastery church of the Holy Cross, and the Rauma congregation moved in. They remembered the collapse of the roof of the Trinity church, though, and to this day there is a belief in Rauma that some day, when the church is full of worshipers, the roof will come crashing down on their heads. At any rate, it probably makes prayer more fervent.

Another plague swept through Rauma. Another fire (the fourth) destroyed the entire city. Hunger, then another plague (the fourth). The Great Unrest, with Peter the Great's armies sweeping through Finland: when it was over, Rauma had seven burghers and six horses.

Actual warfare was not tasted by Rauma until on a warm July day in 1855, during the Crimean War. Word had reached Rauma that the British fleet was attacking all Finnish ports from Viipuri to the northern end of the Gulf of Bothnia. In Rauma everyone hid their wealth under the *sauna* floors and fled to safety to the countryside. The pilots were sent into the country for a vacation, and the Rauma ships were hidden in little coves—with their masts chopped off, it was impossible for the enemy to find them. Two men kept watch in the church tower, night and day, and at last they were able to wave a red flag one morning and cry, "The British are coming!"

The British came, creeping through channels that no one ever used, and at last a British warship anchored in the harbor. A half-dozen small boats, with brass cannon at the bow, were lowered into the water. Everything looked quiet, but suddenly Lindegren, a Rauma merchant and volunteer who had prepared himself for this war by buying ten rifles, fired a shot, and the Russians, hidden in the forest, and the Finns, hidden behind the rocks, began to fire at the six British skiffs parading in the harbor. The battleship opened fire. Two hours later the British retreated.

It was victory for Rauma. Lindegren, who had bought the ten rifles, received a gold cross. Two other men got silver crosses. They were from Alexander II, and they were marked "For Bravery." There was celebrating in Rauma, but it was a bit premature, for three weeks later the British returned. They were more discreet this time; they anchored far out in the harbor. They burned three ships; they set fire to the wooden wharves and storehouses. Nowadays, if someone begins to laugh in an uncontrolled, madman fashion, they say in Rauma that "He laughs like the Englishman when he burned the harbor." The British fired incendiary bombs into the city, but most of them landed in fields or meadows. The curate put a couple of them into a tub of water for two months; after that they were transferred to the Rauma museum, and Rauma went on as though nothing had happened or ever would.

Nothing did happen, except that in 1897 the railroad was built, in 1906 the streets were paved with cobblestones, and in 1934 running water was added to complicate Rauma's plumbing system.

Rauma is contradictory. It concerns itself with such opposite, incompatible elements as lace and the sea, and it is proud of both. It speaks its own dialect, a dialect so hard for an average Finn to understand that it might almost be called another language. It has an old city, with streets too narrow for sidewalks but wide enough for cobblestones. These streets twist in such good medieval fashion that you soon feel you are lost in a maze. If you reach the river, which the people of Rauma call a "canal," you are saved. The harbor used to come up to here, but the sea, as if frightened by the aggressiveness of the Rauma seamen, has retreated and left a meadow. On this meadow the streets are regular, wide enough to have sidewalks and new enough to be dull. Beyond this meadow, and behind the railroad tracks, is the newest quarter. It used to be Rauma's *Kurpark*, with a mineral spring which a century ago attracted flocks of fashionable patients to a regimen of twenty glasses of mineral water before breakfast, meals of porridge and spinach, and evenings of dancing. The ritual may have been too exacting, for the *Kurpark* made room for Rauma picnickers and Sunday crowds. Now, in an attempt to grow, the trees have been cut down, a factory has been planted in the middle, and stakes marking tomorrow's streets are already in place.

In the old quarter, however, you will still find houses that are over two hundred years old, occupied to a large extent by women at least seventy years old. These women are Rauma's lace-makers: all day long they sit in front of a pillow and throw scores of spools left or right, over or under, in a mysterious fashion. The monks first taught this art in the Middle Ages, and by the eighteenth century most of Rauma, men and boys included, used to make lace. Lace was so much on everybody's mind that children, who did not know better, would say "Such *lace!*" when they saw a cobweb on the wall.

The cobwebs are generally neatly swept away, but you cannot brush aside the Rauma language. Everyone is so busy, what with lace-making and going to the sea in their ships, that they have to talk briefly. Every extra syllable, every extra vowel is swept away, and the result is like this: *San snää mnuu snääks,*

snääks mnääki snuu sano. Eleven vowels more would make that intelligible Finnish, and the sentence which looks so threatening would mean "Call me thou, that is what I call thee."

This language is not taught in the schools. It does not have to be—even the schoolboys are in such a hurry to get down to the sea that they speak it by intuition. It is so bad, however, that scholars write learned treatises about the Rauma dialect, but these treatises are generally even more unintelligible than their subject.

The one intelligible force, the one really vital force in Rauma's life is the sea. Rauma has played with the sea ever since there was a sea to play with. It is the core of their existence: *Navigare necesse est, vivere non necesse.* The Rauma war memorial skips the soldier with the sword motif and puts a ship on top of a pedestal. Gravestones replace granite palms with schooners etched on the stone. Ever since Rauma was a city the Rauma ships have sailed the seas with their cargoes of wood. This trading, the core of Rauma's existence, has also given much trouble to the Rauma burghers. Some Swedish kings gave Rauma full rights to sail anywhere they pleased; others told them to keep their ships at home; still others, that they could trade with all cities but Lübeck or with no cities except Lübeck. At the end of the nineteenth century, however, Rauma's fleet was Finland's largest, and in the statistical tables to-day, the port of Rauma is listed immediately after Turku in importance.

Seventy years ago my grandfather left this city for the little red cottage he had built four miles north of the city. The cottage lay on a bluff; there was a meadow in the front yard and a cove behind the house. Grandfather walked to his cottage; grandmother, with a baby in her arms, sat on the cart with the household goods. Later there were more children. Then the three daughters married—their homes are not far away. The two sons went to the sea. One of them returned to the land, married the girl his brother had given up, and settled down to farming on week-days and sailing his yacht on Sundays; the other son went to America. Grandmother died; then, after a few lonely years, Grandfather followed her. The red cottage was sold.

The three sisters still live near the red cottage. They get along well with each other on the whole. but when they quarrel they do it properly and refuse to visit each other for a year or two. Their brother near Turku is generally forgotten, except when he writes, or when his daughter gets a divorce and remarries. This daughter is too much for the three Rauma aunts to understand; they belong to a simpler day. One of the three likes to swear and spend money. The second aunt is parsimonious; she swears, too, but she goes to church regularly. The sea has made her fatalistic: her husband sailed from Newport News on the *Albyn* on a stormy November day in 1920. The ship was not heard of since, and a few months later it was on Lloyd's "black list" as lost. The third aunt, Alina, is political-minded. She is a Socialist by conviction. She is an agnostic, too, except when she writes letters to my father, or reads the Bible secretly on Sunday mornings, or hears of the death of another one of her friends.

Whatever Alina may think of Socialism or God, she firmly believes that Rauma is always Rauma, that, furthermore, what was good enough for her mother is good enough for her. Living with Alina means living the life of a bygone generation. Alina's only concessions to modernity are trading at the co-operative store around the corner and occasionally taking a taxi-cab to Rauma.

Alina bakes her own bread, but more than that, she grows the wheat and rye on her own fields, she harvests it and threshes it in the way it has been done for centuries. Meat comes from the calf or the pig she has fed in her own back yard; the fish on the table are caught by her son-in-law. Alina makes her own clothes: the wool is sheared from her own sheep, washed and carded, spun at home, woven into cloth and knit into stockings. The tablecloths, the sheets and towels are all woven by Alina—after she has grown her own flax in the field nearest the cove. The rugs on the floor are woven from old clothes. From morning until night Alina is busy with a hundred tasks, but she always has time to sit down for a cup of coffee every hour or so and ask me questions about America.

For an American, such a completely self-subsistent existence is almost inconceivable, and, indeed, it is no longer common in Finland. To Alina, however, it is nothing remarkable; it is simply the natural way of life. It is the way life was pictured in the *Kalevala*. Today's newspapers may be on the table, the taxi-cab may be waiting at the door, but otherwise nothing is changed. The rowan tree is outside the door, the birches are not far. The weathered log storehouses are in a row in the yard, and beyond them is the *sauna*.

The *sauna* is one of the most important elements in Finnish life, and one might say, even more aptly than of Rauma, that "the *sauna* is always the *sauna*." The *sauna*, essentially, is nothing but an unassuming building, preferably near water, with a pile of stones and a platform inside. The stones are heated, you sit on the platform, throw water on the heated stones, then beat yourself with a bunch of sweet-smelling birch twigs as soon as the steam fills the

room. The Finnish bath house has been like this a
thousand years, just as it was when Wäinämöinen

> . . . warmed the sauna
> And the stones prepared to heat it,
> And the finest wood provided,
> Water brought in covered vessels,
> Bath whisks also, well-protected—
> Warmed the bath whisks to perfection,
> And the hundred twigs he softened.
> Then he raised a warmth like honey,
> Raised a heat as sweet as honey,
> From the heated stones he raised it,
> And he spoke the words which follow:
> "Now the bath approach, O Jumala,
> To the warmth, O heavenly father,
> Healthfulness again to grant us,
> And our peace again secure us."

God is no longer worshiped in the *sauna*, but it has
been almost as a sacred place, a place where you
would pray to God as in a church, where you would
not be profane any more than in a temple. Mothers
always gave birth to their children in the *sauna*. If
you were sick, the *sauna* would cure you, or nothing
would. If you were well, the *sauna* would cleanse
you, your body would feel as new, and your mind
would be rid of the petty, inconsequential things of
life and full of the worth and goodness of man—it is
no wonder the people in the murals of that Tampere
church are naked: they are ascending into heaven
from a *sauna!*

FINLAND

You do not go to the *sauna* as soon as the embers have died down under the stones. It is left to stand for an hour or two. In Wäinämöinen's day that was so the ancestors could bathe first, but Christian theology explained that the devils should have a chance to gloat in the heat and then clear out. The Finn, though, can probably stand more heat than the devil. Furthermore, it is a sacred place, as Eino Leino described in one of his *Whitsuntide Hymns:*

The Lord walked on the isthmus on a sere August day, and He was tired. He met an old man in the valley, and asked him the way to the nearest house. His legs could carry Him no farther. "Then let the leg break."

He came into a house. Could He find a bed for the night? "On your way, tramp!" replied the old woman.

He asked the farm girl for a grain to eat. "Steal it from the hens!" she retorted.

The Lord heard the beating of bath whisks and knocked on the *sauna* door. "You will let me bathe?"

A contented voice answered Him: "Whoever you are, come in!"

The Lord threw water on the stones and blessed the steam, and the people wondered that it smelled of a thousand roses and hissed from the stones like the music of church bells. And the blind saw, the deaf heard, the crippled and sick were well.

"What is this for a church—black sooty stones? An altar—this bench?" they asked.

The Lord folded His hands across His breast, the walls moved away, the roof arched up: the sky was a tent, the lamps of the Lord blazed in the sky. . . .

That is only one of the mysterious things that can happen in a *sauna*. A similar thing happened to Lönnrot, when his wisdom was almost heralded as something supernatural. It was on one of his *runo* collecting trips through Carelia. The *sauna* at a farmhouse seemed pleasant to him that day, and he recited a poem in thanks to the girl who had thrown the water on the stones and washed his back. When he returned to the same farm a year later, the *sauna* was immediately heated for him. Lönnrot was surprised at the unexpected hospitality, but he went cheerfully to the *sauna*—followed by two girls from the next town. He looked at them, but they sat stubbornly in the corner and would not stir. Lönnrot threw water on the stones and beat himself with birch twigs. He looked up; the girls were still there. He stared at them, but they did not stir. Finally he asked them what they wanted.

"Recite us your poem," the girls said, "the one you spoke last time in this *sauna*—that girl got a husband right away."

Lönnrot recited the poem, and the girls left the room satisfied. Unfortunately Lönnrot did not have time to find out if they, too, got husbands.

In Helsinki there is an elaborate *sauna,* with

swimming pools, women to massage you, coffee to drink in between steamings, scales to weigh yourself before and after. That is fine, of course, for the urbanite and the curious tourist, but the Finnish *sauna* is a little red building on the edge of a lake. Inside there are dark wooden walls and a simple platform, a pile of heated stones and bath whisks in the corner. Here children are born and the sick get well. Here the stains of hard work are washed away and the body and soul refreshed.

When you stand in front of Alina's *sauna* to cool yourself in the breeze, you can look across the cove to Grandfather's red cottage on the knoll fringed by tall pine trees. Most of Grandfather's life was lived in that cottage: there he always came back after the long cold days supervising the workmen in the forest; there he saw his children grow up, wave goodbye and leave. And when he was gone, a young family moved in one spring: the husband walked, the wife and two children rode in the wagon full of furniture, beginning a new cycle.

My father was born in that cottage. Here he lived and went to school, rode honey-colored horses with flaxen manes, skated on that cove, went to Rauma on errands, went into the forest with his father, read aloud to him in the evenings—the Bible, *Ensign Stål,* the *Arabian Nights.* When he was not quite old

enough, he went to sea in his uncle's schooner, looking for adventure. When he was not much older, he
came to America, leaving that cottage as his brother
and sisters had left it.

Three weeks before my father's birth, the girl
who was to become his wife was born in Virrat, north
of Tampere, at the end of the Poet's Way.

This Näsijärvi boat trip has actually received this
name because Runeberg lived on the shore of the
lake for a time. Against my better judgment, I began
to feel a bit "poetical":

> Pleasant 'tis in boat on water,
> Swaying as the boat glides onward,
> Gliding o'er the sparkling water,
> Driving o'er its shining surface.

The clouds were fleecy, billowy things. The sun
sparkled on the water. Rocky shores and dense forest
alternated with meadows sloping to the lake.

Down on the lower deck someone was playing an
accordion. Tired-looking peasants were sitting in the
stern, crowded in between the bicycles, the sewing
machine, the miscellaneous kegs and barrels, a dog,
a cow sniffing at a chaise longue and a sack of
flour. On the upper deck it was hardly better.
Most of the people were tourists intent on seeing
what there was so remarkable about the Poet's Way.
One old man followed every twist and bend with

atlas in hand, others read the guide-book descriptions of the beauties of the trip so avidly that they forgot completely to look up and see the beauty. A Danish lady was making a needlepoint chair cover for her husband's study; one woman was occupied with a three-pound novel in her lap. I escaped to the bridge. The captain was an old friend of mine—he had learned to pilot a ship in Rauma, he had sailed the seven seas, and for twenty-five years he had gone up and down the Näsijärvi.

For miles we sailed on a broad lake, then wound through straits, went step by step through a lovely canal whose shores were decorated with lawns, flowerbeds, trees and garden walks. The lake grew broad again. We rounded an island and came to Ruovesi, which is a town with meadows sweeping down from the church hidden on a tree-crowned hill to the lake. Here Runeberg lived for a year as a tutor; here he met the old soldier who became Ensign Stål. Runeberg had a favorite birch tree he used to climb on summer evenings—so many people have climbed it since, that now it has been fenced in, as befits a shrine. He had a favorite forest pool, deep in a glade —on a January day a flock of swans flew over the pool, and one of them came down to swim across the water and sing a melancholy song—the people did not learn until afterwards that Runeberg had died on that very day.

It is to Ruovesi that the people of Keuruu, some forty miles away to the northeast, used to come to church, arriving in their long church boats, like huge canoes, with sixteen oars and thirty-two people pulling against the waves. These people of Keuruu were Pirkkala merchants, too, and were strong-minded men. They did not come to church often. Once, however, they started for church a week ahead of time, fortified with several kegs of strong beer. Several days and nights they spent in their forest inn on the way, and the kegs were emptied. They arrived at Ruovesi in the highest of spirits. They marched into the church, decided not to take their own pews in the back of the church but went straight to the best seats near the pulpit. That led to a grand fist fight in which everybody joined. The Keuruu men won and sat down as if nothing had happened. Their punishment came later: for one whole year they had to stand during church services. It seems they did not learn their lesson, though, for a few years later, in 1562, the Turku bishop declared that Keuruu was the most godless parish in all Finland and excommunicated the whole parish for a year. Perhaps that is why my mother's ancestors left Keuruu and moved to Virrat, which is called the loveliest township in all Finland.

Virrat has a monoply on pastoral charm: everything seems soft and rounded: the forests, the mead-

ows, the lakes. It has a church on a hill-top, and behind the church the cemetery slopes down to a lake,
with weeping willows on the shore. It has a tree-
lined main street, rich farms, and—so that people
will not think that perhaps this is not Finland, after
all—it has memories of Finland's greatest bear hunter
(he was a small fellow, a weakling in his youth,
but he killed one hundred and ninety-eight full-
grown bears and thousands of cubs) and it has a mysterious lake, long and narrow and dark, with high
cliffs along one side, which some have compared to
the Styx, and others, more romantically minded,
have called "Love's Altar."

My mother has never seen this "Love's Altar."
Perhaps she was considered young; perhaps it was
because she always got seasick on the boat trip to
Virrat. Besides, one only went to town for important
matters, like going to church. My mother's home,
Vilamo, is some fifteen miles from the town, and
going to church meant a two-hour walk, a three-hour
boat trip in one of those long slender church canoes,
and long monotonous hours in the church itself. It
is not on record that the family went more than once
or twice a year.

To make up for this deficiency, rural Finland had
the *kinkerit,* a peculiar institution: the curate, his
two assistants and the sexton visited each village of
the parish once a year, stopping for a day at one of

the houses in the village and seeing how well the villagers knew how to read. It was a celebration, from all points of view. The big houses of each village took turns in being hosts. When the *kinkerit* came to Vilamo, Aunt Mimi would dash to Tampere for delicacies that were not available in Virrat, and there would be cooking and baking and cleaning for a week before the day finally came. The churchmen came late in the afternoon, brought by their host of the neighboring village. The sexton used to come with his own horse, for he was a poorly paid man and had a chance to get his horse fed at someone else's expense. The gentlemen were in high spirits, but by the next morning they would be sober. They had to be, for a hundred men, women and children, the aged and the very young, would fill the huge kitchen of Vilamo. Everyone was served coffee and cake, and then the curate would say a prayer and baptize the children born since his last visit to the village. The boys and girls who were ready for confirmation were taken to another room, and all the rest of the people lined up in families, waiting for their names to be called: the wealthy families first, of course, and then on down the social scale. The curate asked each person to read aloud a bit from the Catechism, and then to explain the meaning of the text. When everybody had been "read," the poor people went home, and the rest stayed to a big banquet.

FINLAND

They ate cheerfully, because they could forget their Bibles for a year—until the next *kinkerit* came around. After that the curate, his two assistants and the sexton wrapped themselves up in the carriage and went on their way to the next village, for they would hold the *kinkerit* there the next day. On the way the gentlemen would drink enough so that they arrived at their destination in high spirits.

Dances at Vilamo were more popular, and Grandfather did not need any excuse to call in a couple of musicians and invite the village to dance. Soon the big kitchen would be filled with couples. It is here that my Uncle Sem met Mimi, the young school-teacher who had come up from Tampere. It was love at first sight. She stayed on as governess for my mother and her sisters, and then she married Sem. After that there were fewer dances at Vilamo, because Mimi disapproved of them.

It was a lonely life. Christmas came but once a year, work almost every day. Neighbors were far away; it was too far to go to school. The loneliness was so depressing that Mother's younger sister, Enne, married a man twice her age: he had courted all six of the Vilamo sisters, and he finally got the youngest one. After Enne got married, Mother came to live with her married sister in America.

One day at Vilamo, poking through the books

piled in high stacks in the guest house, I found a
slim book with my mother's name inside. It was a
school-book, and most of it looked pretty dull. There
would be a story about a princess, then something
informative, an anecdote with a neat moral attached
to the end, and then another story about a prince, a
great battle, life in pagan Finland, or a description
of the Finnish winter or summer—which should have
been obvious enough without being put in a text-
book. There was also a story called "The Fairest
Province":

There was once a gallant warrior who won so great
a victory for his country that his king said to him:
"Pick yourself the best and fairest province of Finland, and it shall be yours forever."

The soldier thanked his king and sailed to Finland, but when he stepped ashore at Rauma he was
puzzled. "Which way shall I turn," he wondered, "I
do not know this land at all."

"Why not go to the market-place, my Lord,"
prompted the captain of his ship. "There is a fair in
the market-place today, and people have come together from all the corners of the land."

The soldier made his way to the square in the
center of the city, plodded through the gay crowds
and pushed his way to the platform in the center.
"Stop!" cried the soldier, and the uproar slowly died
into a murmur. Curious faces peered up from all
sides. Whispers began: who was this stranger? why
had he so suddenly ended their business and merri-
ment? what did he want of them?

FINLAND

"Tell me, people," cried the warrior, "which is the best of all your provinces. I am looking for the man who can show me the fairest province of Finland."

The crowd hesitated, murmured, and searched for its voice.

"My Lord," a short lithe man dressed in a leather suit came up and spoke, "it will be impossible for you to find a fairer province than Lapland. It is far in the north, crowned with high mountains and surrounded by broad rivers. You will find the Arctic seas, broad marshes, steep fiords, and far distant views. Don't you know about our rushing rivers, our gold, our silken furs? In summer the sun rests above the horizon day and night for week after week. In winter there is no sun at all, but the northern lights flash their gleam across the sky. Take Lapland, for it is certainly the best of provinces."

"Impossible," asserted a man standing in the middle of the crowd a scowl on his face, his legs widespread, his hand on his puukko, "What is there in Lapland besides mosquitoes and howling wolves? I advise you to pick Ostrobothnia if you want a huge fertile land. The level fields are covered with wheat; the harbors are full of rich ships with cargoes from Visby and Bremen."

"And what do you pretend to know about the sea?" a sailor quickly demanded. He turned calmly to the warrior: "If you have the courage and the daring to fight the sea, choose Åland. You will have gray rocky cliffs by the thousands, green islands, white sails, and bright waves. Nothing can compare with Åland."

A gardener laughed at the Ålander. Leaning on his hoe, he addressed the warrior: "Åland? Åland?

Do not let any good-for-nothing sailor give you his
choppy seas and barren rocks! You want a land with
good harbors, rich chains of islands, trees heavy with
apples and cherries. You want a province where
every city is like a page from an ancient chronicle.
You want the Hundred Communes."

"The time is past when the Hundred Communes
were best," a proud landowner informed the crowd.
"By all means choose Newland if you are looking for
the best: the finest lace and beautiful maidens, green
fields and rich estates—"

"Ho ho! hear that!" laughed a man at the edge of
the crowd. "Newland, indeed! Why, it fits into one
tiny corner of Carelia! Do you want the land where
the sun rises? a land between two seas? hundreds of
hills and valleys, lakes and rivers? the fastest horses?
Then take Carelia and hear our minstrels sing of old
enchanters, sing the magic songs of the land of
heroes."

Finally an old man shook his head. "What is all
this talk about the seas? What do you say to a land
where you can sail your boat for hundreds of miles,
following the birch-covered shores of one lake and
then another? If you searched the land with a candle
in your hand you would find no fairer province than
Häme. Such fields of flax! such green fields you will
see nowhere else!"

The brave warrior laughed. "I have heard enough.
How can I choose the best, when each province is
best in turn? I will ask my king for a hill-top in the
Hundred Communes, overlooking the sea and the
sky and a thousand islands. There the sturdy New-
lander will build my castle. The men of Åland will
sail my ships; the fields of Ostrobothnia will give
wheat for my bread. I shall buy the finest linen of

Häme and the warmest furs of Lapland. The Carelian will sing me songs of heroes. Friends will come to me from all the country. Have I chosen correctly?"

"Well, now, who can dispute it?" an old woman asked her neighbor, and the whole crowd agreed.

Scene: America.

It was one of Christine's successful evenings. A big house on a hill-side, the candles flickering merrily through the big windows of the music room, the light pouring over the lawns and gardens and colliding with the glistening row of automobiles that filled the drive.

I no longer remember the music, only the sense of well-being, the enthralled faces (and Woodby's pudgy, puzzled one—fidgeting and wondering why he had allowed himself to be snared), glowing eyes, the slightly overheated rooms, Etand's slender fingers on the keyboard, the shadows of candles flickering on the carpet—and Mrs. Smith.

Yes, Mrs. Smith: a tall, thin woman in gray, a parson's wife with a slightly radiant, embracing manner, Christian and all-loving. (Mr. Smith, tall and gray, too, was hovering somewhere in the background, probably lost in thoughts of how his morning's sermon could have been less gaunt and gray, more radiant and all-loving.) Mrs. Smith beamed as she reached my corner. One had space for breathing there, for the others had not found it. I bowed and mumbled my name, but the words rolled away and were lost in the hubbub of voices discussing Music and Life with a metallic finality. Another attempt: now Mrs. Smith was puzzled. Was I Bohemian? she beamed. No. French, then?

"Ah, Finnish!" she glowed when I told her humbly. "But then you must tell me your story." I did not know there had to be a "story," but I got as far as my birth. Then Christine appeared, and I joined the circle of Music and Life. But I did not forget Mrs. Smith: she beamed again as I passed by with ice and cakes for Ann, she nodded as we sauntered by to the terrace, and she caught my arm just as Mr. Smith was taking leave of Christine. "I am sorry you could not go on with your story. But you know, you are so fortunate in being Finnish."

"Fortunate?"

"There is no glamour in being Anglo-Saxon," she sighed.

I looked surprised.

"No, absolutely no glamour," she sighed, seeming to regret the everydayness of being Mrs. Smith, seeming to envy me because I had some connection with Finland.

There is no reason why Finland should be glamorous for me. Surely you know that Finland is not an ice-bound fishing village on the Arctic, with polar bears running in the lanes. Nor do wolves howl at the door-step and claw the children to pieces. The people are not haunted with the specter of eternal ice, gloomy darkness, hunger, oblivion. No, it is a bright land of vivid blue and rich green, sparkling white, and practical red paint. A land where a people have worked hard, centuries long, to earn independence and peace.

I accept my parents' coming from Finland just as I accept my being born in Fitchburg, Massachusetts. Is there glamour in either fact? I speak Finnish because we speak it at home, just as other people might speak German or French or Chinese. I go to a *sauna* on Saturday night, because it is a natural thing to do—but then I suddenly awaken from my matter-of-factness to come closer to the Finnish spirit when I feel the moist heat and the aroma of birch leaves in my nostrils. With that ritual, with its incense of heat and birch leaves, the body glowing with moisture, comes a sense of well-being. And to me there sometimes come misty remembrances—how much of it is memory? how much the quiet reminiscing of my parents when some book, a picture, an unexpected letter, or just the moment has evoked the mood?—remembrances of a time when I was a boy in Finland.

I was five years old at the time. The trip had a good beginning: a few happy months—Father and

Mother at the warm seaside laughing and throwing me into the water in spite of Grandmother's loud-voiced protests. Christmas, with my red stocking cap borrowed by a shy schoolboy for his part in the school play; a tree with garlands and fruit. Grandmother's stories. A toothache. War—long months of privation, with Mother growing thin, and worrying and growing thinner still as I became ill, desperately ill. The snows melted and the spring rains transformed the placid brook in front of Grandfather's house into a raging torrent. All summer bright-uniformed Cossacks rode madly over the brook and along the highway. More privations, then America.

The return did not end my unhappiness. The other boys on the street called me "Bolshevik." Was it because of the red stocking cap? or was it something deeper? Perhaps because there had been a war between the Reds and the Whites, and my father had casually declared that the Reds were not barbarians. Perhaps it was simply because I had forgotten English and spoke only a strange, foreign language.

Seventeen years—and Finland again. With a mustache and a neatly trimmed beard that made me appear ridiculous—only Irmgard was polite enough to say I seemed like a "foreign-looking intellectual." I remember more from this trip; I was impressionable and flippant. I looked at everything with tongue in cheek: at cities, at lakes and fields, at people. I remember Olga and Albertina, long conversations about Finland for the Finns, and the lakes and the forests and the northern night. . . . The other day Oiva showed me a letter I had written him at the time: "At last I left Frankfurt, with lovely farewells and too much wine and a bronze satyr and trying to see Irmgard but not much succeeding, and now I have been in Finland for weeks: Helsinki, Rauma, Virrat, Tampere, Svonlinna, Viipuri and Rauma, Rauma, Rauma. . . . These provinces—charming, simple, refreshing, naive, healthy, godfearing, de-natured alcohol-drinking, puukko-stabbing—plus the mysterious midnight sun, warm days, heavy food, monotonous food, still more food, widows and children, and for me about half a hundred cousins and a sprinkling of aunts. . . .

"When I get back to America I shall write an article, to wit: Words of Wisdom, or the travelers' aid; or, how to travel about penniless, spending twice as much money as you plan to spend; or, hotel bedrooms but why ring for the maid; or, how to see a city from the leading bar and avoid sightseeing; or why hurry through Germany, but Finland in summer is lovely and warm but cold and rainy if you leave your raincoat at home but an Irish Tante will come to give you cognac and aspirin, English cigarettes and good advice gratis so why worry, or is a country inhabited by the natives, for the natives, or in spite of the natives, oppression, tyranny and the love of God. . . ."

I felt at home in Finland, but I longed for America, for New York, for a hill-top in Vermont. And when I returned I did not write the article; I forgot about the words of wisdom. One wintry afternoon I might have begun, but I remembered Christine's musicale that evening and knew that nothing would come of the article. Then Mrs. Smith smiled her way into the corner where I was beginning to mutter, "Oh God—"

"No, absolutely no glamour," she sighed, with that faint bourgeoisie longing for adventure in her heart she would never satisfy. She would never be able to stand naked in front of the *sauna,* with the cool breeze meeting her warm body, and remember, dimly, vaguely, a night and a day that had been somewhere far off, remember listening to wizened old men and pipe-smoking old women telling tales. . . .

Perhaps that tale of the gallant warrior who won so great a victory for his country that his king said to him: "Pick yourself the best and the fairest province of Finland, and it shall be yours forever."

How was the warrior to choose? He did not know the land, and when he came to the market-place, each one in the crowd praised his own province as the best and the fairest.

I cannot make the choice for that gallant hero. I have tried. But Rauma, the home of my father, is still the fairest of cities, and Virrat, where my mother was born, the loveliest of towns.

Of that I am certain. It is all fresh in my mind, for I have just seen Finland. Not because it is bizarre or thrilling, faraway or strange (except perhaps for Mrs. Smith). Or even romantic, though for me it holds romance: Finland is the country my parents left to seek life in America, to seek the fulfillment of their desires. There is nothing unusual in that, but for each new-comer it has meant the unique experience of ending a life and beginning a new one. And between that end and that beginning there has been a sigh for the old—of relief, perhaps of doubt or pain, always of longing. A part of that sigh has become a part of me. Let me search frantically for Irmgard in Frankfurt, or stand in Times Square, or on a hill-top in Vermont, yet I remember that I have a heritage, a silver cord that both frees me from the old and draws me to it. I have been to Finland to see the country my parents first called home; I have tried to capture that sigh (is it pain? is it longing?) which is hidden in the breast of everyone who has ended a life and begun a new one.

LAND OF HEROES

Thou hast here a lovely village,
Finest spot in all of Northland,
In the lowlands sweet the verdure,
In the uplands, fields of beauty.

Fare ye well, ye streams and lakelets,
Fertile fields, and shores of ocean . . .
Fare ye well, dear scenes of childhood,
Happiness of days departed.

INDEX

INDEX

268

INDEX

270

INDEX

The Finns, a people who look fearlessly
to the morrow.

The republic farthest north rises from the sea,

like Helsinki, sparkling and gay, to live intensely

the summer freedom which knows no night but
the twilight-dawn of pale shadow.

There was winter once, and oppression, jealous
Russian eyes ruling from the Big Square;

there was freedom, too, for a summer: Finnish land,
a Finnish building, Finnish laws.

Between the southern coast

and the Arctic wasteland,

from the east

to the western shores

lies the Northland:
"In its lowlands sweet the verdure,

"In the uplands, fields of beauty."

The pioneer looks about him:

between the forest

and the lake

he builds his home. The wilderness is conquered.

The forests are cleared, crops planted, harvests
stored for dark winter days.

A village appears;

like Porvoo, grows into a town with
cobblestone streets;

like Virrat, builds a church;

like Tampere, shelters poets, to sing Finland's
song, to sing of the fairest province and the
bravest heroes.

To me, Rauma is always Rauma, the
fairest of cities;

Virrat, the end of the Poets' Road, the
fairest of towns;

the Finns, a people who look fearlessly
to the morrow.